Sexuality and Dating

Saint Mary's Press
Christian Brothers Publications
Winona, Minnesota

Sexuality and Dating
A Christian Perspective

by
Richard Reichert

Nihil Obstat: Msgr. Roy E. Literski, PhD, STL
                Censor Deputatus
                August 1, 1981

Imprimatur: †Loras J. Watters, DD
                Bishop of Winona
                August 1, 1981

The nihil obstat and imprimatur are official declarations that a book or pamphlet is free of doctrinal error. No implication is contained therein that those who have granted the nihil obstat and imprimatur agree with the contents, opinions, or statements expressed.

Sexuality and Dating: A Christian Perspective is intended for use in conjunction with the Student Guide for Personal Reflection, under the supervision of a teacher employing the approach outlined in the Teaching Manual, and with the written permission of the students' parents.

Illustrations: John Arms, pages 81, 105; Edward Bock (Photo Library), cover; Laimute E. Druskis (Editorial Photocolor Archives), page 99; Rohn Engh, pages 78, 85, 93; Therese A. Gasper, page 28; James C. Gehrz, page 33; Joel Gordon, pages 7, 17, 20, 23, 27, 37, 46, 50, 53, 58, 61, 64; Clemens Kalischer, page 71; Elizabeth M. Nelson, pages 15, 38, Nancy Palmer Photo Agency, pages 2, 31, 43; Norman Provost, FSC, pages 24, 45, 66, 89, 108-109; Shelly Rusten, pages 56, 94; Andrew Sacks (Editorial Photocolor Archives), page 49.

Third Printing—1985

Edited by Stephan M. Nagel

ISBN: 0-88489-133-X
Library of Congress Catalog Card Number: 81-51011

Contents

1

SEX Is a Nine-Letter Word

The speaker on the steps of the Senate building is working the crowd to a peak. Banners and placards are everywhere. The crowd is orderly but intense. At the signal from the speaker they break out in a rhythmic chant. Over and over they chant and the volume swells. It is a rally urging the lawmakers to support women's rights. *Being male or female is more than biology: it is also culture, politics, and values.*

On a dingy downtown street a neon light flashes on and off in the late night gloom...Massage Parlor...Massage Parlor. A well-dressed, middle-aged man approaches, gives a furtive glance around the street, and then quickly enters. *Being male or female is more than biology: it is also a matter of choices.*

A young couple sits in the waiting room of a rather plain-looking office. They are obviously nervous. Conversation is limp. They keep glancing toward the door to the inner office. After what seems an eternity, a woman appears in the doorway holding an impressively thick file of paperwork. She smiles warmly at the couple and announces, "You have been cleared to adopt. We will have a baby girl for you in twelve weeks." *The desire to parent is more than a physical instinct.*

Across town another young couple sits in a similar looking waiting room. Same nervousness. Same halting conversation. Same glances at a door to an inner office. A man in a white coat appears and announces, "The arrangements have been made. You are scheduled to report to the clinic tomorrow at 9 A.M." It is an abortion clinic. *Through circumstance, ignorance, selfishness, or fear we can be motivated to make radical decisions contrary to our basic instincts.*

A young boy gives his hair one last careful touch with his hand and then rings the doorbell. Scurrying inside. Voices. His stomach does a slow turn. The door opens. A girl in a light blue formal appears, smiling nervously. It is the first real date for both of them—and it is not going to be easy. *Discovering how to relate as male/female calls for some courage.*

The clan is laughing and teasing one another as they assemble for the picture. Fidgeting young children are held in position. The middle-aged couples take up a position in the back. Younger couples, holding infants, stand in front of them. A tot's yellow cap is put back in place for the third time. At the center of all this joyful commotion an

elderly couple sits calmly, smiling smiles of deepest contentment. They are holding hands. She has a rose corsage. She is radiant. He has a carnation in his lapel. He beams. The group is celebrating this couple's fiftieth wedding anniversary. *Discovering that you are lovable and loved takes a lifetime of giving life.*

We Are Sexual Beings

Many single-celled organisms can reproduce themselves **asexually.** This means that these lower life forms are not divided into male or female. For most higher life forms, however, this is not true. In these life forms the reproduction and consequently the survival of a given species depend upon **sexual** reproduction. Each species is, therefore, made up of two biological groups, male and female. Both the male and the female are essential if there is to be any reproduction.

Frequently we take for granted the sexual nature of higher life forms. An individual animal is either male or female. One's **gender** defines what biological role the individual must play in reproducing the species.

We humans share this characteristic with the animal kingdom: we are male and female. Both genders have an essential part to play in the reproduction of our species. The drive or instinct to reproduce is one of the strongest we possess. The very survival of the human race depends on it.

Yet that is where our similarity to other life forms ends. Our sexuality, our maleness or femaleness, involves choices. We can choose to pursue the physical pleasure in sex as an end in itself, totally divorced from reproduction—or even relationships. The existence of massage parlors is rooted in this fact, as are pornography and masturbation. On the other hand, as humans we also can choose to recognize sex not just as physical pleasure, but as a special expression of love.

Yet a fundamental orientation of our sexuality is toward reproduction. Even if couples are physically incapable of conceiving, many still desire their physical union to be fruitful in some way. So they turn to adoption in order to fulfill this desire to give life to another human being.

Being a man or woman involves us in much more than reproduction though. Our gender gives us a fundamental orientation toward all

reality. Our self-images, as well as the roles, expectations, and limits society places on us are largely rooted in the fact that we are male or female. The women's rights movement is seeking to remove some harmful roles and unjust limitations, but the fact remains that our gender will continue to affect how we experience all aspects of life— and how we are treated by the society we find ourselves in. Without a doubt we are "sexual beings," male or female.

When we observe a couple celebrating fifty years of marriage or a young boy and girl venturing out on their first real date, we are observing another very important facet of being sexual. Men and women are attracted to each other for more reasons than sex. We find people of the opposite sex attractive emotionally, intellectually, spiritually. In fact, men and women need each other in order that each can achieve personal maturity. Physical mating is just one aspect of a much larger picture when it comes to being a sexual person.

An all-male or all-female society would be sterile in more ways than reproductively. While religious communities of men and women are dedicated to the Gospel ideal of celibacy, they recognize that their psychological **wholeness** and even their personal **holiness** require healthy, supportive relationships with persons of the opposite sex. We know from the Gospels that Jesus' closest, most loving friends included both women and men.

Learning to relate in wholesome, helpful ways with members of the opposite sex is an essential and lifelong task we all face. The first, tentative steps are usually awkward, filled with embarrassing moments. *(I don't dance very well. Will he/she notice the zit on my chin? What do we talk about?)* Such efforts become complicated even more by the presence of our genital sexual instincts and urges.

Learning to exercise responsibility for and control over these physical instincts is also a major task in youth—and throughout life. It is the lack of such responsibility and self-control that is often the cause for the many unwed parents, abortion clinics, broken marriages, and the currently epidemic number of venereal disease cases. How we begin to deal with our genital sexual instincts when they first appear can set the patterns we will follow throughout adult life. At times self-control can seem like the most difficult task. The stakes are high, however. Our capacity to bring into existence new human beings is one of the most awesome powers we possess.

But learning to deal with your genital sexual capacities needs to be kept in perspective. It is only one of the tasks involved in becoming a mature person. It is only one aspect of your *sexuality* (that's the nine-letter word).

In approaching this course, try to keep that in mind. Being a sexual person involves our total experience of reality. It involves our total **person**. We are so much more than a set of genitalia with an urge to "do it." We came into this world male or female—and God saw that as good! That means that we have gifts and talents to develop and share, friendships to forge, and many other ways to express our sexuality besides sex itself.

Getting the Facts About Christian Faith

There is one other important point to keep in mind before we begin. As you might imagine, this course is rooted in the Christian moral tradition. Unfortunately, that tradition has received a lot of bad press, especially in our times. In popular opinion it is often viewed as oppressive, negative, out-of-date, anti-sex, and anti-pleasure. "If it feels good, it must be a sin" is how too many people summarize the Christian position on sexuality and sexual behavior. In fact, there have been some distortions of Christ's teaching which deserve criticism. But if you get enough of the facts, you will discover that the teachings of Jesus are anything but negative or anti-sex.

For openers, Christians believe it was God who created us male and female, who gave us our physical instincts to mate, and who attached so much physical and emotional pleasure to the sexual acts related to reproduction. If sexual acts and sexual pleasure were evil in themselves, they would not have been in God's creative plan.

Moreover, Jesus certainly did not go around condemning such things. In fact, as we will see later, Jesus was what can be termed a true sexual revolutionary. Today's so-called "sexual revolution" is not actually a revolution at all. Sexual license and promiscuity, "musical bed partners," pornography, perversion, and prostitution are as old as the human race. Any history book dealing with former civilizations can demonstrate that. Our contemporary society did not invent such activities.

Jesus, on the other hand, is a true revolutionary because he is the first to recognize and teach the full meaning and potential of our sexuality and our genital sexual activity.

We will not be making direct references to Jesus' teaching in the early chapters of this course, since so much of what we need to know about ourselves and our sexuality is within the range of common sense and reason. But please keep in mind that it will be Jesus' teaching that underlies all that is presented. His revolutionary teaching actually begins where our common sense and reason leave off. That is why we must ultimately look to him to discover the full meaning of our sexuality—as well as our existence.

What to Expect in This Course

To help you get some idea of how this book develops, here's a brief summary of what the following chapters contain.

Chapter 2—Don't Blame the Stork
Here we deal with the importance of getting the facts about the biology of the human reproductive system and human reproduction. It is not an "everything you wanted to know" chapter as much as it is an opportunity and a call to check out what you already know, discard the half-truths, and fill in any gaps you might experience in this crucial area of self-understanding.

Chapter 3—Male *or* Female
Boys and girls are different in more ways than just their physical make-up. Some reasons why and some information about how they are different form the bulk of this chapter.

Chapter 4—Male *and* Female
Here we get into the fact that all of us are actually both male and female on the psychological level. Integrating these two aspects of reality into our own conscious lifestyle is a critical part of achieving maturity as a person.

Chapter 5—Dating Is Different from Mating
One of the more common and potentially more important forms of boy-girl relationships is dating. What dating is really all about, how to approach it, and how to grow from it are the main topics of this chapter.

Chapter 6—What's Happening?
Here we check out the present scene, how society views sex and sexuality—the society in which you are to develop as a person. It stresses the importance of getting a perspective. It was not always "the way it is."

Chapter 7—The Rest of the Story
Jesus is a true revolutionary. His views about sex and sexuality are truly revolutionary. We will explore the nature of that revolution in this chapter. Believe it or not, Jesus is pro-sex.

Chapter 8—But Is It a Sin?
Just what is the Christian position on things like non-marital sex or masturbation? How far can I go? Actually that is the wrong approach. It might be better to ask: What am I called to become as a human being—male or female? Principles for personally deciding if you are becoming more or less fully human will be discussed.

Chapter 9—Waiting for the Preacher
How do you stay straight when everyone and everything suggests non-marital sex is okay "if nobody gets hurt"? How do you deal with your sex drives—or someone else's—on a date? if you really love each other? if you really do want to wait until marriage?

Chapter 10—Until Death—and Beyond
This final chapter seeks to bring all the other chapters back into some kind of focus. Just what does it mean to be a fully integrated sexual person? What about celibacy as a way of life? Where does it all end up anyway fifty years down the line? in eternity?

That is pretty much what we will be covering. Glance ahead at some of the other chapters if some topic or other interests you. But be sure you end up reading **all the chapters.** Each depends on, and helps you to understand, the others.

FOR REVIEW
1) Explain the difference between *sex* and *sexuality* in our lives.
2) Why is Jesus said to be a true revolutionary?
3) Define: *asexual reproduction, sexual reproduction, gender, pornography, masturbation, evolve.*

God created man in his image; in the divine image he created him; male and female he created them.

God blessed them, saying: "Be fertile and multiply; fill the earth and subdue it. Have dominion over the fish of the sea, the birds of the air, and all the living things that move on the earth" (Genesis 1:27-28).

2

Don't Blame the Stork

Imagine an alien, some Mork-like character, comes to earth on a mission to discover the nature of sexuality and genital sex in the human species. Imagine this alien gathers his information from only three sources: public lavatories at bus stations and schools, slick magazines like **Playboy,** and certain TV situation comedies and R-rated movies. His report back to his planet might go something like this:

"The human body is rather unique. It comes equipped with certain organs which humans use as toys to derive pleasure. The male 'toy' is on the outside of the body, and it seems the larger the toy, the more pleasure it gives. There is much talk about size.

"The female's main toy is hidden inside the body, but the female does have two additional toys on her chest. Again size seems to be very important.

"There seems to be no end to the ways with which humans can play with these toys and to the games they have invented for using them. They have many strange names for these toys and games. In many of these games the boys talk about 'scoring.' Some games can be violent or painful, I believe, given the names they go by.

"One very popular game is called 'making love,' but it seems to

have little to do with the emotion they call 'love.' It has more to do with 'making,' but I am not sure just what it is they make. Sometimes they simply refer to 'making it' or 'making out,' rather than making love. They also refer often to 'doing it.' According to the bumper stickers and T-shirts I've seen, there is no end to the ways or places for 'doing it.'

"I had originally thought these games had something to do with reproducing the species, but from the sources I have studied so far, there seems to be no connection between these games and human reproduction."

Unfortunately, there are many earthlings whose knowledge of sex and sexuality is nearly as limited as this imaginary report. This very limited understanding of humanness and sexuality fixes on only one aspect of it—**orgasm** and related physical pleasure. Such a narrow view results in a distorted and dehumanized view of our sexuality and our genital sexual behavior. Sexuality is reduced to an it, as in "making **it**" or "doing **it**." Sex no longer seems to involve people at all. Genital sex is, in fact, reduced to a game, where success is measured in terms of "scoring" or where the goal is "going all the way." The genital parts of our body, God-given and marvelous, are reduced to tools or sports equipment or weapons and are given vulgar, mechanical names. It is as if our genitals were detached from the rest of us—separated from our personality, our intellect, our values, our emotions. They are viewed as instruments of pleasure, toys, and the pleasure they provide is viewed as an end in itself, almost totally removed from human relationships or reproduction.

Sex for most people is just one of many interests that occupy their time and energy. Yet for too many people, when their interest does turn to "sex," it is this depersonalized, orgasm-seeking interest.

You might rightfully object that you and many of your peers do not approach your sexuality in such a dehumanized way. Agreed! The fact remains that many people do (boys perhaps more often than girls), and as long as this is the case, you yourself are in danger of being influenced and manipulated by these popular and ever-present concepts. For that reason, there is no better remedy than knowledge—accurate knowledge of what it means to be a male or female human being. It seems the most logical place to start is with the biology of your own body.

Who Needs Sex Education?

Sex education, meaning education in the biology of the reproductive systems of the male/female body, is dealt with differently in each culture. Each approach reveals something of that culture's overall attitude toward sexuality in general.

It is curious to note, for example, that in an atheistic country like the USSR the general population of adults are tragically ignorant about much of common sense biology regarding human reproduction.

In other countries, where sexuality is strongly identified with being **macho** (male chauvinism), the teenage male first receives his "sex education" when his father brings him to a house of prostitution.

The Victorian era of nineteenth-century Europe, which greatly influenced attitudes in the United States, approached sex as a kind of "no-no," as a necessary evil, and as a burdensome obligation for a wife. There was virtually no public discussion of the topic, and what

education there was usually was offered just prior to—or even after—marriage.

Our contemporary society gives the appearance of being very up-front about genital sex. It is dealt with openly in the press, in TV dramas and documentaries, and in many movies. Almost every newsstand carries popular magazines and books that are sex-oriented. "How to" books are often bestsellers and available to anyone who can afford to buy them.

But that is not the whole picture. Just as often we can find groups and movements seeking to ban certain books, films, TV shows. The topic of sex education is almost always hotly debated whenever it comes up on the agenda of any local school board. Certain locales, in fact, have banned all sex education courses.

Yet both the "anything goes" and "any knowledge is too much" approaches to sex education are defective for the same reason. Each approach fails to deal with genital sex and human reproduction *within the larger picture*—along with our bodies, human sexuality embraces our intellect, emotions, spiritual values and insights, personal identity, personal relationships, and social roles.

The net result of these two conflicting approaches in our society is that they cancel out each other. The "up-front approach" has too often succeeded in creating a limited or distorted interest in genital sex alone.

For that reason, teachers of just about any subject must choose their words carefully. Even the most harmless phrases and traditionally wholesome words are often given some kind of sexual connotation by many students and produce giggles, smirks, and knowing glances. For example, look what has happened to the word **gay.**

The "censorship approach" gives necessary information the appearance of being forbidden fruit and actually intensifies our hang-up with genital sex. Imagine someone drawing a circle on the ground and saying, "Now, if you step into this circle, you will be in big trouble." "What's in it?" "Never mind that. Just don't step in it or else!" If you are like most people, you find it extremely tough not to step into the circle. At the same time this approach too often succeeds in keeping necessary information away from those who need it the most—teenagers who face the task of learning to integrate this new physical capacity into their lives, their persons, and their personal relationships.

So, on the one hand, many young people develop an excessive curiosity about facts that are as natural as facts on good nutrition. On the other hand, they are often deprived of the kind of accurate information they need and deserve to have provided. Or, just as bad, even when they have the accurate information, it is viewed out of the context of the whole picture because of society's preoccupation with genital sex rather than sexuality.

Where Do You Fit into All of This?

This chapter does not intend to give you a detailed course in the "facts of life." The reason is simple enough. There is no way of knowing just how much good information you have already received in other courses like biology or in special programs designed specifically for this purpose.

Also, the written word alone is impersonal. Any information given should be given in such a way that you also have opportunity to discuss it with concerned people like your parents and teachers. So it will be up to you, your parents, and your teachers to work through the facts if you need to do so. But, here is a little test you can take to give you an idea of just how much you do know—and more importantly—how you typically feel about this knowledge.

INSTRUCTIONS:

Below is a list of words and phrases that deals with biological facts related to the human reproductive system and human reproduction. Read each word on the list, and then ask yourself the following questions regarding each: (No writing is necessary.)

a) Could I give a good factual definition or explanation of this biological term? Try it.

b) Would I feel any embarrassment using this term in talking with adults or peers when the biology of human sexuality is the legitimate topic of conversation? Why or why not?

c) How many "street words" do I know that are used for any of these terms (e.g., street words for the female breast)? Why are these street words usually considered "dirty" in polite society whereas the listed words would be acceptable?

1) sex organs, genitals, puberty, secondary sex characteristics
2) ovary, ovum, menstrual cycle, menstruation, menarche
3) testicle, sperm, spermatozoa, scrotum, penis
4) Fallopian tubes, uterus, womb, vagina, hymen, clitoris
5) ovulation
6) ejaculation, nocturnal emission
7) copulation, genital intercourse, coitus
8) orgasm
9) conception, conceive
10) contraception, contraceptive(s)
11) impotence
12) fertility, sterility, surgical sterilization, tubal ligation, vasectomy
13) pregnancy, pregnant
14) fetus, fetal development, zygote, embryonic sack, embryonic fluid, umbilical cord
15) miscarry, abort, miscarriage
16) abortion, abortifacient
17) premature, trimester, full-term, Caesarean, breech birth
18) mammary glands, breasts
19) hormones, estrogen, testosterone, FSH

How Did You Do?

If you feel that you cannot explain many of these terms, do not be surprised or embarrassed. For all the supposed sophistication about sexual matters in our society, there are many adults who would have problems giving some terms an accurate definition or explanation.

Also, this list does not contain "everything you need to know but are afraid to ask." It just contains the basic terms related to the biology of human reproduction.

What about the second question? Do you find any of these words embarrassing? Ask yourself, why should these words cause any more embarrassment than words like *lung* and *breathing*, *vein* and *bleeding*, or *appetite* and *eating*? If they do cause us some embarrassment, the usual reason is that we are still uneasy about the fact that we are sexual beings. This uneasiness can be caused by many things. Can you think of some reasons?

What about the street words? These are the slang terms many young people and adults use in discussing matters related to the biology of sex and human reproduction. Just as often certain physical organs and reproductive functions are used in insults, like "You dirty

_____." Or "Why don't you go _____." You can fill in the blank with just about any of the street words you recall.

Slang words have been with us a long time, and every culture has its own set. We must grant that they are often much more vivid than some of the scientific terms. But they imply assorted misconceptions about our reproductive organs and their functions. Or they are derived from a concept of sexuality that reduces it solely to genital sex and orgasm. For example, one street word for conceiving or being pregnant is to be "knocked up." Did you ever stop to think what a distorted, narrow, or ignorant expression that is for the miracle of human reproduction?

Go through the street words you know and ask what kind of concept or attitude toward sex and sexuality they suggest. Words reveal thoughts and thoughts reveal the person. That is the discouraging thing about the popularity of the street words used to discuss human sexuality and genital sex. If, for whatever reason, you do not know the biological words and their meanings, you should learn them so that your knowledge of the human body and its functions is at least scientifically accurate. And if you often use street language as a handy tool for insulting others, you should realize that, by doing so, you help deepen distortions about sexual matters for both yourself and others.

The giggles, smirks, and knowing glances that sometimes spread through a group when a word like _gay_ or a legitimate reference to a breast or penis is mentioned usually indicate a natural embarrassment about sex and the adult body you are now acquiring. But the more comfortable you can become with precise terms and expressions, the more you will be able to avoid the many mistaken notions regarding sexual matters.

Fantasy Island Doesn't Exist

A side effect of the distortions about or ignorance of our reproductive systems is the creation of various myths and misinformation surrounding the whole topic.

1) For example, you need accurate information about physical development not only in what is happening to you individually, but also what is happening to members of the other sex. Girls, for instance, reach physical maturity first, beginning at ages eleven or twelve. Boys

begin reaching puberty a year or two later. No two people go through the rapid physical changes on the same schedule, however. Some start earlier; others later. As a result, you might find yourself well ahead of your friends physically or lagging behind. In either case, it can be an uncomfortable or embarrassing situation for a year or so.

Not only do we go through puberty at different rates, however. We also end up at different finishing points. Very few boys wind up with the huge-boned, heavily muscled, hairy-chested bodies that win a coach's attention. Nor can many girls acquire the contradictory "full-bodied, but somehow slim" shape labeled beautiful by teenage magazine and advertising writers. It is a painful but fortunate fact that most of us have to look more than skin deep to find our confidence and identity.

2) For example, too, you should be informed about conception in some detail—precisely how it can occur, the capacity for a sperm to find its way to an ovum even when not deposited directly in the vagina or during the fertile period. It is often moral weakness joined with ignorance rather than gross immorality that accounts for so many teenage unwed mothers (and an equal number of unwed fathers) each year—to say nothing of abortions. One study shows one in ten teenage girls will get pregnant before age 18. And three of every ten pregnant teenagers get an abortion. The more you know about the kinds of risks people are running when it comes to "doing it," the more it can help in making the decision to search for the best sort of sexual relationship. Likewise, there are as many myths about how to prevent conception as there are regarding how conception takes place. But we will deal with the question of **contra-conception** a little later.

3) As another example, the medical community keeps warning us that there is a virtual epidemic of **venereal diseases** among teenagers. (These are diseases which are contracted, in almost all cases, during genital intercourse.) The reason for this is not just increased numbers of sexually active young people in our society. It is also plain ignorance and myths like, "Only prostitutes and lower class people get VD." There is ignorance about the long-range results, particularly permanent brain damage, sterility, and birth defects. There is the widespread myth that penicillin can cure any form of VD, when in fact certain strains are becoming immune to penicillin. Few people know just how many

forms of VD there are (seven major types), how they can be transmitted, or the symptoms for early detection. One doctor noted in a recent issue of a national news magazine that if people were aware of some of the forms venereal disease takes, it "would set the sexual revolution back seventy years."

Good information is necessary even if you are convinced not to become sexually active. Families do not plan to have fires in their homes, but they are still encouraged to identify exits and hold occasional fire drills, just in case. Not as many young people set out seeking to become sexually active as we are led to think. Nor is sex ever an "emergency." But sex between teenagers does tend to be unplanned which means one or both persons may be uninformed or misinformed about the physical risks involved.

Our society, with its preoccupation with genital sex on the one hand and the hush-hush approach on the other, has spawned many other myths related to the topic. There are myths regarding the importance of the size of the sex organs, regarding turn-ons, potency, the effect of alcohol. The list goes on and on.

Probably one of the most widespread myths resulting from our preoccupation with genital sex concerns the supposedly high frequency of intercourse. Ironically this myth is common not only among unmarried people who can only imagine what goes on, but also among married people themselves. Many couples wonder if they are sexually "normal" in regard to their frequency of intercourse.

According to one recent and reputable study, among people married three years or longer, couples have intercourse on an average of two to three times a week (not three times a night as is suggested in the porno magazines). What is even more revealing, though, is that this same research found that couples on an average spend a total of **24 minutes a week** involved in intercourse—or about 8 minutes per event. That includes all the "getting in the mood" and "afterwards" time! For all that people talk about sex, most do not actually spend much time at it, it seems. We spend about 5½ hours eating each week and about 49 hours each week sleeping, yet we seldom talk about these activities. Would you agree that society has blown this one biological function—genital sex—out of proportion?

These few examples are intended to convince you that it is very important for you to get the facts. Do not allow yourself to be misled by all the popular misinformation that is picked up from your peers, from the media, from hearsay and myths, from "men's" magazines

and their female counterparts. Your body and the human reproductive process itself are too precious and important to be clouded by half-truths, street words, myths, and fantasies. Above all, do not be embarrassed to admit there are things you do not yet know, even though it is presumed by your friends or by adults that you know the score.

How do you get the facts? For openers, this course is a useful forum for asking serious questions and for getting some straightforward answers. What you actually need to discuss in the course can best be decided by you and your teachers and your parents. It is a good opportunity for you, so use it well.

Talking with parents can be a little embarrassing for you—and for your parents too. But if you feel you can talk with your parents, by all means do so. Then there is your doctor, a school counselor, a teacher, a parish priest. If you have an older brother or sister who is mature and responsible, that is another good source.

So getting the biological facts is usually well within your reach right now. But when getting the biological facts, keep in mind that they are only one aspect of the much larger question of human sexuality. We need the biological facts, but we need much more. We will look at another dimension of our sexuality in the next chapter.

FOR REVIEW
1) What single aspect of sex do our popular notions center on?
2) What are the two common approaches to sex education? Explain each approach briefly.
3) Why do slang terms often create difficulties in understanding sex and sexuality?
4) At what ages do boys and girls begin entering puberty?
5) What percentage of teenage girls become pregnant before age 18?
6) How many major types of venereal disease are there?
7) According to the study cited, how many minutes a week does an average couple spend having sexual intercourse?

So the LORD GOD cast a deep sleep on the man, and while he was asleep he took out one of his ribs and closed up its place with flesh. The LORD GOD then built up into a woman the rib that he had taken from the man. When he brought her to the man, the man said: "This one, at last, is bone of my bones and flesh of my flesh" (Genesis 2:21-23).

3
Male or Female

In recent years the Olympic committee has found it necessary to give certain tests to female athletes to determine if they are in fact female. It seems some countries give their female athletes male hormones to help them develop certain muscles and to increase their physical strength. By overdoing the hormone injections, some of the women are actually judged to be "male" even though they are biologically female in terms of sex organs.

Also in our time, sex change operations have become more frequent. Individuals seeking such operations—including men who were husbands and fathers and women who were wives and mothers—often complained they felt they were trapped in the wrong kind of body.

Bizarre events like these, when they are joined to the highly important movement to achieve equality between the sexes, have raised questions our ancestors presumed they knew the answers to. Just what does constitute maleness or femaleness? Is it hormones? Is it sex organs? Is it a state of mind? To put it another way, just what does it mean to be male or female? Are male and female in fact equal in all respects apart from sex organs? Are male and female "identity" and male and female "roles" things that are actually learned rather than things that we inherit by being born biologically male or female?

At first these questions may seem strange. Yet how we answer these questions determines to a large degree our personal identity, our behavior, and our relationships with others, both male and female. It is important, then, to get some accurate answers to these questions if we are to become integrated, happy, and self-respecting men or women.

Stereotypes: Music, Print, and Mental Litter

You may have heard this story. A father and his son have a serious auto accident one night coming home from a basketball game. The father is killed outright. The son is critically injured. In the emergency room the staff calls in the best surgeon in town to perform some extremely difficult surgery to save the boy. The doctor, on arrival, takes one look at the boy on the operating table and says in a trembling voice, "I can't operate. That's my son." How is this possible?

That story has been used a lot to illustrate just how sexist most of us actually are. People come up with all kinds of possible answers instead of the obvious one: the doctor was the boy's mother. In a male dominated society it is presumed that the "best surgeon in town" is a man. Most doctors are men. Certainly all the "really good" surgeons are men. It is taken for granted.

It is precisely this kind of **prejudice** and **sexist stereotyping** which the women's movement seeks to challenge. Hurricanes were first named after women because of similar stereotyping. Hurricanes are unpredictable in their behavior, and women have been stereotyped as having the same trait. Hence female names were given to hurricanes until the women's movement succeeded in having the Weather Service name them after both men and women. (Some people even wanted them called "hisacanes," but that might be too much.)

As the women's movement points out, such stereotyping has far more serious effects than merely being insulting. Deeply rooted stereotypes have resulted in all kinds of political and economic injustice. Until the twentieth century, women were not allowed to vote in this country because of the stereotyping that implied they were not logical enough or intelligent enough to be entrusted with voting rights. Until recently it was also a generally accepted practice that women would receive lower pay than men for doing identical work. Women were systematically passed over for positions of authority in business, in

"Of course, our girls' athletic program needs a slightly bigger budget."

politics, at universities, and the like—even though they were often better qualified than the men who received the appointments. Much of this still goes on today, but progress has been made in terms of education and legal statutes that oppose this continued stereotyping and discrimination.

An unfortunate side effect of the women's movement, though, has been to bring about in some people the false impression that equality of opportunity and equality before the law for both sexes mean there are no differences between men and women except the rather accidental differences in their sex organs and in their biological roles in reproduction.

In point of fact, men and women do think, behave, and react in different ways (not better or worse) precisely because they are men or women. Knowing why this is so and just what some of these differences are is important both for understanding yourself and your male/female counterparts.

Human Growth and Behavior

Various areas of research regarding both the development of human individuals and of the human race have begun to reveal significant differences in the ways males and females behave in regard to sexual matters.

1) The most obvious male/female differences that affect sexual behavior are rooted directly in the male/female sex organs. With regard to the male, the fact that the sex organs are external, outside the body, results in the male being stimulated more often. Besides that, experts say that the young male is aroused more quickly and with less stimulation. Also, the male involuntarily experiences an erection about every 90 to 120 minutes while awake or asleep, simply because hormones are periodically released which trigger this physical reaction.

All of this suggests that there is some biological basis for the observed fact that a male often is more easily and more frequently "turned on" than is a female. Nature seems to be constantly priming the healthy young male for procreating, that is, for creating new life and for continuing human life. For the individual, however, this natural drive can be a source of frustration.

In the case of the female, the sex organs are more protected and are not as subject to touch or stimulation. Also, it appears that it requires more stimulation before full arousal takes place in a female. This does not mean, however, that girls do not get aroused, and it does not mean that such arousal cannot sometimes happen involuntarily with no apparent stimulation. Research merely suggests that females are not biologically primed for genital sexual activity as frequently or as rapidly as are males. A failure to recognize this difference can not only cause embarrassment and misunderstandings between teenagers on a date, it can even cause serious marital difficulties.

2) Research has also shown that biological sex is determined at the moment of conception. It is decided by the combination of **chromosomes** in the female ovum and the male sperm. Once sex is determined by the match-up of chromosomes, a whole set of other processes that affect the developing fetus is set in motion. It is interesting to note that, for the first ten days or so, the fetus is essentially female in structure. After that time, if the fetus is male, certain hormones are then produced that control the development of the male sex organs. If the fetus is female, the female sex organs are similarly developed through certain hormones.

Recent studies further suggest that these hormones not only serve to develop the appropriate sex organs, but also influence the development of the brain. The differences are minor but not insignificant. For example, growth in that portion of the brain that controls the emotion of aggressiveness is stimulated by the male hormone. It is, therefore, slightly less developed in the female brain. This can be demonstrated by observations of humans who have suffered an imbalance in the proper hormones. As a result, some researchers claim that the male child tends to be more aggressive precisely because he has a more aggressive brain, due to different hormones that affect growth.

3) As mentioned above, people experience both strong drives toward reproduction as well as powerful stimulation connected with intercourse (orgasm). This sexual instinct is second only to the instinct to survive. Thus nature guarantees the continuation of the human species.

Furthermore, this is an instinct which we share with mammals— from which we clearly evolved. So by studying in mammals the male

and female roles in reproduction, we can learn more about certain distinctly male and distinctly female kinds of behavior.

As one example, among mammals the female can produce very few offspring compared to other varieties of animals. So the survival of her offspring partly depends upon how well the female selects its mate. The female who can select a strong and healthy mate can best insure healthy and strong offspring. To illustrate, a wild mare will not accept just any stallion that comes along. The stallion with whom she mates must prove itself by defeating other contenders or by manifesting bravery or cunning. Given our evolutionary history, can we find this same "strategy" at work in female human beings? Some researchers think so. Humans, after all, have to cope with the same problem: How do we insure the survival of relatively few offspring? In fact, women do value strength, bravery, and intelligence—although we also tend to value love, concern, and fidelity for other reasons which are uniquely human. We will discuss those reasons shortly.

Following this line of study, then, we find that girls are less often promiscuous than boys and are not as often interested in short-term relationships that center only on genital sex. A girl first tends to seek a loving, lasting relationship, and only after the relationship is satisfying does she become interested in genital activity. Until recently our culture has reinforced this instinctual approach while, at the same time, it has built many false stereotypes around it.

Returning to studies of the mammal, we find that the male's problems are quite different. The male produces over a hundred million sperm in a single ejaculation, and it is biologically equipped to replenish this supply every few hours. The male mammal's chances for reproducing itself, then, lie in numbers. Obviously the more females he impregnates, the better his chances that one offspring will survive and be healthy. From a chipmunk's point of view, then, quantity is as important to the male as quality is to the female.

As with females, we find that this instinctual approach to sex is not entirely lost in human males. Boys tend to be more promiscuous than girls and more often approach sex as an impersonal activity—a "numbers game." The kind of "love 'em and leave 'em" attitude with which we stereotype human male sexual behavior may well have some biological and historical source because, **for lower animals,** it helps assure the survival of a species. In humans, however, there are overriding values which we will discuss next. What's important in what has been studied and guessed at here is that, again, humans seem to approach sex quite differently depending on whether they are male or female.

4) From the same biological drive discussed above—the drive to reproduce—we may also find a basis both for the traditional importance placed on marriage and for the traditional "double" standard with which society has treated men and women differently and often unfairly.

The human offspring—and usually there are more than one in a family—takes many years of developing before it is capable of taking care of itself and surviving on its own. During much of that time, especially in the child's earliest years, the mother needs a great deal of help. Historically women have had to care for infants almost constantly. So in the hunting and food-gathering societies from which our present cultures emerged, a father was needed for more than impregnating the woman. He had to be willing to help out after the birth—to hunt, to ward off dangers, to gather food. Without such assistance the children would die. As a result, it seems that a strong tendency toward "pair bonding" slowly developed in which both human mates cooperated in raising their offspring.

In this arrangement, however, one last difficulty presented itself. Infidelity on the part of the woman could not be tolerated. Only the strictest rules of fidelity offered the male any assurance of the children actually being his. How could he be sure he was not working, hunting, gathering food, and risking his life for years to support some other

man's offspring rather than his own? Even suspicion of infidelity became acceptable cause for punishing or leaving the woman.

Thus, say some researchers, the double standard emerged in history and is today deeply entrenched in all kinds of unjust stereotypes. "A man can fool around, but a woman cannot." "Boys go out with bad girls, but they marry good ones." A boy can have the reputation of being quite a "stud" and it is a mark of distinction. A girl, on the other hand, gets the reputation of "being loose" and becomes a social outcast.

Are you beginning to get the picture? There really are differences between males and females. Even as we continue to question and debate such research and the ideas it has generated, it appears that our sexual behaviors and reactions are to some degree influenced by the fact that we are either males or females.

Because we also possess an intellect and a free will, however, we are not enslaved by these instinctive reactions. We have the capacity to direct our thinking and our behavior by powers greater than the biological instincts and the evolutionary conditioning we have inherited. But recognizing that we have such instincts and have been conditioned by evolution is a big step forward in understanding ourselves as males or females—and toward understanding our female or male counterparts.

Pink or Blue?

Some college students once performed this experiment. They dressed a nine-month-old baby in what were obviously boy clothes: a kind of football jersey, baseball cap, pants. They took the child to a busy shopping center and observed how different people reacted to the child. Then they took the same baby, dressed it as a girl with a bonnet, frilly dress, bows, and the rest. Again they observed. When the baby was dressed as a boy the passersby would say things like "Hi, tiger." Or they would give it a playful pat or tussle. Dressed as a girl the same baby got reactions of cooing, "Oh, how sweet!" and the like.

The experiment served to demonstrate just how early a culture begins to impose its stereotypes and sex roles and expectations on its young. Actually it begins in the hospital with blue or pink identification cards.

As we suggested, many of these sex-role stereotypes do have some basis in the biological differences of males and females. But at best stereotypes are just that—exaggerations, oversimplified descriptions of a reality—half-truths. Just as often stereotypes have no basis in reality.

As we are now beginning to discover, for example, there are virtually no occupations within our society that cannot be done equally well by either women or men if they receive the proper preparation and training. Stereotyped sex roles do not hold up. Men can do an excellent job raising children and tending the home while the wife pursues a professional career. This is a common practice in Sweden.

What about things like pro football? some will say. Well, if girls in our society were forced, like most boys are, to get into physical contact sports very early and to develop the kinds of muscles those sports demand, there is no biological reason that women could not eventually match their male counterparts in skill or performance. They can even be trained in the aggressiveness they do not naturally possess.

In many countries, for example, Russia, women work side by side with men in the most physically demanding kinds of labor. Women have also proved to be very tough, effective combat troops in countries where they are expected to serve in the military.

You are being asked to keep two things in mind, then. On the one hand, there is a real biological basis for what can be called a *male*

identity and a *female identity*. "Male" behavior and "female" behavior, or male and female reactions, do exist. Your personal identity is (or should be) rooted in physical maleness or femaleness. That's what you are—and it is good.

On the other hand, much of what is called typical male or female behavior, attitudes, skills, or characteristics is rooted in exaggerations and cultural stereotypes that have no basis in reality. Men and women are actually much more the same than most past cultures realized or wanted to admit.

In the next chapter, we will take a look at the human consciousness men and women share. It too is a very important part of becoming a fully integrated person and understanding your sexuality.

FOR REVIEW
1) What injustices does the women's movement seek to correct?
2) Why do boys experience sexual arousal more often than girls?
3) Explain this comment: "From a purely biological view, quantity is as important to the male mammal as quality is to the female."
4) Describe the biological and historical basis for the traditional *double standard.*
5) Define: *prejudice, sexual stereotyping, chromosomes, instincts.*

In Christ the fullness of deity re-
sides in bodily form. Yours is a share
of this fullness...(Colossians 2:9).

4
Male and Female

The ancient Hebrews had a religious practice involving what they called
a scapegoat. Each year during their season of penance the high priest
would gather the people together. They would admit all their sins of the
past year. The priest would lay his hands upon a goat as a sign that the
sins of the people were now placed upon the goat. The goat was then
driven out of the camp and into the desert. The symbolism is clear. The
people's sin was rejected and removed from their midst.

Too frequently we hear how some person or group of young
people break into a school on a weekend and virtually destroy the
place. If you have ever seen the results, your first reaction is that it was
done by crazy people. The senseless destruction of expensive and
useful equipment and facilities boggles the mind. Psychologists tell
us that many young people doing this kind of thing are lashing out in a
symbolic or imaginary way at powers and forces (the establishment)
against which they otherwise feel powerless. The things they destroy
are in a sense their scapegoat. Obviously, this does not justify such
action, but it at least helps us understand a little better what at first
seems to be insane behavior.

Just about everyone these days complains about the violence on TV, including pro football. The primary complaint is that it tends to corrupt the young and to fill their minds with violence, making it seem natural or desirable behavior. There is much evidence to support the arguments too.

On the other hand, some point out that such imaginary violence, and even the real but "disciplined" violence of a sport like pro football can serve a very useful purpose in society. Anger, aggression, and even rage are all natural emotions for us humans. When we experience one of these emotions, we need some form of outlet for it.

In our society there are all kinds of restrictions on expressing emotions like anger. If a classmate really gets you angry, you are not supposed to start a fight at the first chance you get. So what do you do with the anger? If the boss gives you a bad deal, cussing at him or her, or even telling the boss what you think, could mean you lose your job. Again you are stuck with the anger.

That is where the violence of TV or pro football can serve some purpose for some people. It gives us a vicarious or imaginary outlet.

The bad guy who finally "gets his" in some violent way in a TV drama becomes in our imaginations the classmate or the boss, often unconsciously. But the angered person will sometimes feel better and the anger will go away after such a vicarious experience. Seeing the opposing team soundly beaten by your favorite does the same thing. This is not an argument for more violence on TV. It merely helps explain why people often enjoy violence on TV or in films.

You've Got One—An *Unconscious*

By now you are wondering what all this has to do with a course on human sexuality. Actually a great deal. What you experience consciously—thoughts, ideas, fantasies, certain emotions—is just a small part of what is actually in your mind and constitutes just a small part of who you really are. There is a whole other dimension to you that dwells in the unconscious part of you but is just as real and plays just as big a part in what you do.

Much of what is in your unconscious you have inherited, and it is common to all us humans. Some of its contents are there because

they slip in from the conscious part. What slips in may be wonderful images or ugly things, or it may be things that at the moment just do not seem important enough to think about. All kinds of impressions are filed away in the unconscious.

The trick, of course, is to make conscious as much of the unconscious part of us as we can. Then we can deal with its contents properly. When our thoughts remain unconscious, they come out in disguised ways we often have no control over. Many times unconscious thoughts or feelings are expressed in ways dangerous or harmful to us and to others.

For example, if the vandals who use a school as their scapegoat could just name the cause of their unconscious rage (a teacher, a failure, a school rule), then they could deal with it more rationally. Destroying a school may make them feel better for a moment, but the real cause of their rage is still there. So is the damage.

Another example. Did you ever notice that the people you most instinctively dislike will often—on a closer look—have certain unpleasant traits that are very much like your own. He or she is your scapegoat. It can be easier to dislike those traits in someone else than to admit you have them yourself. Often you will dislike a person because he or she is reminding your conscious mind of ugly things about yourself that you have hidden in your unconscious.

There are other ways our unconscious feelings slip out that are less dramatic—and often unrecognized. Dreams often reveal to us what is in our unconscious. But dreams are usually highly symbolic expressions of our unconscious and can be hard to interpret.

For example, probably all of us have some time or other experienced a dream in which we were being chased by some awful person or creature. The fear we experience is actually an unconscious fear that we have within us. The monster chasing us is a symbol expressing whatever it is we fear—and it is not always easy to determine what the symbol actually means. It may be some person or event from our childhood that we no longer think about. It may be something current which we are unable or unwilling to face consciously. Accurate interpretation of dreams can often be a real help to us in naming and dealing with feelings and images floating around in our unconscious. You might try recording your own dreams in a journal for a while.

Not everything in our unconscious is bad or ugly. In fact, much of it is very good and important to us. Some researchers say that our best part is actually within the unconscious and needs to be gradually brought to consciousness. And that is where we get back to the question of our sexuality and our identity as a male or female.

All of us, males and females, have both a male and a female dimension to us. The identity that **first** develops in our consciousness **for the most part** corresponds to our gender. A male becomes consciously male first and a female becomes consciously female. That is no surprise because it is what society and family and friends expect of us. But what many people do not realize is that there is a feminine dimension to each male that lies in the unconscious. Likewise, each female has a masculine dimension within her unconscious. Just as our **sex**uality means we are male or female, the human **person**ality includes both dimensions.

At the start it must be stressed that we are not talking about homosexuality. We are explaining how psyches are made up. Also, be on guard—as we talk about the feminine consciousness or the masculine consciousness—to avoid the trap of the stereotypes we mentioned in the last chapter. We are talking about aspects of the human mind, not people. We are talking about different *starting points* or different *orientations* that exist within every human personality.

For example, it is a fact that what is termed "feminine consciousness" is oriented more toward persons and relationships than toward things and goals. This does not mean that women are not interested in things and goals. It does mean that a woman's **starting point** tends to be persons and relationships. Other characteristics of the feminine consciousness—being careful not to stereotype—include a capacity to put together complicated details and get to the heart of the matter. The feminine consciousness is not illogical but is often able to get to the real issue almost instantly. The female consciousness also tends to be more receptive, open, compassionate, gentle, sensitive to feelings, less interested in competition, and more interested in harmony.

The "male consciousness" tends to reflect the opposites—again being careful to avoid stereotypes. The "male consciousness" is more interested in things, tasks, goals, the practical. It is logical and generalizes more than it intuits. Generalizations are logical models of reality

WHAT DID YOU SEE FIRST IN THIS DRAWING? Some people see a vase first, while others see two faces. At a simple level, this trick drawing demonstrates the fact that any two people can look at the same object and each see something entirely different because their *starting points* are different. Once we become aware that there are two alternative images here, our minds shift back and forth between them.

and can remove us from it. Intuitions, on the other hand, remain very much in direct contact with reality and are not subject to logical analysis. For this reason, an intuitive person can often drive us crazy with illogical conclusions. Yet those conclusions will often end up to be more accurate than our logically formed generalizations. Remember, all of us are quite capable of intuition, but the initial male orientation is toward the logical and the generalization.

The "male consciousness" is more competitive, aggressive, impersonal, less interested in feelings of others, and more interested in getting the job done. It tends more toward justice than compassion, is less open to new ideas unless they are logically presented, Is a taker rather than a receiver.

One Plus One Equals One Hundred Percent

Given these two starting points within the human mind, society over the centuries has tended to reinforce them in a million ways. Females are expected to be passive and males aggressive. Mothers are expected to maintain the family with love, gentleness, and compassion, and the father is expected to go out into the jungle or to bring home the bacon.

Boys are not supposed to cry. They are supposed to be tough, competitive, brave. Girls are expected to look pretty, and it is okay for them to cry and express fear. Boys play football. Girls relate to the crowd as cheerleaders.

In fact, any male who begins to show any trait of what has come to be considered female consciousness—like sensitivity to the feelings of others—is immediately suspect. Any girl who is too aggressive, too hard-nosed, too competitive is considered out of line. Research has revealed the fact that by the end of high school most girls have given up competing even in school work. As a result, women's IQ scores begin to drop.

What all this fails to realize is that lurking in the unconscious of each of us are those same qualities and capacities that we normally associate with the opposite sex. *Culture* **demands that we keep them down there unless we want to be considered queer.** *Nature* **demands that these qualities become part of our consciousness and our conscious behavior so that we can grow and become mature.**

That is what the male/female relationship is ultimately all about. Each gender can help the other become whole. Each can help complete the other. We need each other for much more than just the biological reproduction of the species. We need each other if we are to reach our full potential as individuals.

Just on the level of consciousness the male and female make a good team. Typically when a couple is looking at a house they are thinking of buying, they go in different directions and notice different things. The woman might tend to be thinking "home" and check it out in terms of living space, comfort, cheeriness, attractiveness, or its potential to be made attractive. She might ask questions like where will the nursery be, how cozy is the kitchen, and such. She is culturally conditioned for this approach.

The man for his part might check out the roof, the furnace, the plumbing, workspace, general condition. He might be thinking "house." He is culturally conditioned for this task.

This kind of "divide and conquer" approach actually results in a rather complete check on the potential value of the house. It is a good example of how the male and female orientations and consequent cultural conditioning can complement each other and result in a decision that is much better than one made by only one or the other.

Obviously there is no reason a woman could not be knowledgeable about plumbing and roofs. Many are. Likewise, men can have a good eye for the potential homeyness of a house. The important point, whatever their starting points, is that they share their insights and combine their judgments in coming to a decision. *Helpmating* **is the name of the game in successful marriages.**

But the male/female relationship is actually intended to go far beyond this kind of pooling of each other's conscious talents. Ultimately, it can bring **our own unconscious** maleness or femaleness into our consciousness so we can accept it and use it. That is when we become a whole person in both the psychological and the sexual sense of the phrase. How does this take place? It begins with that special form of projection we call falling in love. It ends—it is to be hoped—with an authentic love relationship through which each partner becomes a whole person.

Let Your Partner Do the Walking

We have seen that we sometimes project our unconscious fears or undesirable traits onto a scapegoat. Falling in love or **infatuation** is in a sense a kind of scapegoat experience in reverse. What we often first find attractive in another (once you get beyond physical appearance which may either attract or repel) are actually those appealing qualities in the other which lurk **in our own unconscious** but which we have not yet been able to make conscious.

Did you ever hear the expression, "opposites attract"? Often it happens that some big, rough, loud type of fellow ends up marrying the sweetest, most gentle and polite woman you could imagine. Underneath all that conscious macho within the guy lie all those unconscious qualities of gentleness and kindness that are so visible in his wife. Fearful of revealing that side of himself, he is able to experience the other half of himself through projection. His wife acts out the unconscious qualities he is unable consciously to admit he has.

Such an extreme case serves to illustrate what is at work in all meaningful relationships between boys and girls, but often in a more low-key, less obvious way. We tend to fall in love with or to feel a strong attraction to those persons of the opposite sex who most seem to reflect openly our unconscious other half, including the male or femaleness within our unconscious. That is why it is so often impossible to account for love, to explain it, to define it. It is rooted initially in the unconscious and brings with it powerful feelings of attraction. (We are not talking about those superficial attractions we feel toward a beautiful girl or a handsome boy.)

If the "falling in love" relationship blossoms into authentic love and tends toward a permanent relationship, what was at first unconscious in us becomes more conscious. A rough, tough boy takes on gentle qualities and is not embarrassed by it. A quiet, meek girl becomes more self-assured and assertive. Each helps bring out the potential that had been hidden—and often repressed—in the other. The partners create each other, make each other **consciously** whole persons. What actually happens is this. Our partner helps us to learn to love and to be comfortable with our **whole personality.** Once we love ourselves, we can afford to love the other unselfishly, for the good the other possesses. In other words, the first step in the love relationship is to help the

other to discover his or her own lovableness. We will talk more about that in the next chapter.

"What Did He Say?"

This is difficult stuff. As you are beginning to see, being male or female, a boy or girl, and learning about "sex" is much more than asking "how to do it" or "is it a sin?" Sexuality goes far beyond our sex organs. It goes to the very depths of our unconscious and to the very heights of our consciousness. It involves every aspect of our beings and all our relationships, not just those involving genital sex acts. There is much more at stake than avoiding pregnancy or maintaining a good reputation and a clear conscience. Our understanding of our sexuality affects our personal identity, our capacity to love ourselves and to love others, our sense of self-worth and self-respect.

That is the real danger for those that limit discussion of sexuality to genital sex or obtaining orgasm. They miss the true meaning and full potential of our sexual nature.

For now just keep in mind that there is another dimension to you hidden in your unconscious. It is your maleness if you are a girl. It is your femaleness if you are a boy. It is good, it is holy, and it eventually has to become a conscious part of your personality and your behavior if you are to become a sexually and psychologically whole person.

Our cultural conditioning teaches us that there would be something wrong with us if we let that part of us out in public. Don't buy it! That has been one of the biggest mistakes ever forced upon us. And it is one of the key reasons our sexuality so often does get limited to a focus on genital sex, orgasm, and sexist stereotypes—the most primitive, obvious, and instinctual level of our sexuality. That is all animals have. But we are not just animals. We are humans and our sexuality plays a much larger role than reproducing the species.

If you want a good example of a truly sexually integrated person—one in whom the masculine and the feminine were given full, balanced, integrated expression in consciousness and behavior—take a good look at Jesus in the Gospels. Both men and women publicly and unashamedly loved him. Why? Because in him they found fully developed and visible the masculine or feminine qualities hidden in their own unconscious. He brought out the best in everyone, both men and women. By loving and being loved by him they themselves became

whole—sexually, psychologically, spiritually. This freed them to love others authentically.

Take some time to reread this chapter and think about it. It is heavy, but it is worth the trouble for you. What we have discussed may help you to understand—in a positive way—the overwhelming feelings of infatuation you may be experiencing or have experienced already.

FOR REVIEW

1) What is a scapegoat?
2) What does the human unconscious contain?
3) Why do women tend to develop a *female consciousness* first, whereas men tend to develop a *male consciousness* first?
4) How can male/female relationships help us to develop more fully human personalities?
5) Define: *vandalism, vicarious, helpmating, infatuation, projecting.*

Your love must be sincere. Detest
what is evil, cling to what is good.
Love one another with the affection
of brothers. Anticipate each other in
showing respect (Romans 12:9-10).

5
Dating Is Different from Mating

Cartoonists seem to think it was pretty easy for a man to get a mate in prehistoric times. All he had to do was zonk the woman of his choice with a big club and drag her off by the hair to his cave. Even today it is the custom among certain cultures for the man to stage a mock kidnapping of the woman he seeks for his wife. It is civilized in that arrangements are made ahead of time between the two families and the man and woman involved. But this "caveman" approach is an integral part of certain marriage customs.

Each culture throughout history has developed its own methods of matchmaking. Though some might seem very primitive to us, many are still practiced today. In some instances, the man and woman were promised to each other by their parents as infants. The first time they meet is sometimes on the wedding day itself.

Oftentimes marriage has been more a business or political deal than the final coming together of two lovers. In some cultures today the father virtually "sells" his daughter to the suitor offering the best price. In other cultures, it is the bride who must provide a "dowry" to give to the prospective husband.

In our own culture, we presuppose that boys and girls will freely

associate with one another from early on, date whom they choose, and eventually marry whom they want to marry. Many parents have little to say about whom their children in the late teens date, and parents certainly have no real control over whom their children will marry once they become of legal age.

Actually this is rather new even in our culture and in the world at large, going back not much more than fifty years. Before then most boy-girl social events were group events and they were usually sponsored (and carefully chaperoned) by adults. One-to-one dating was considered "courting" and begun as the young people neared adulthood. It was taken for granted that marriage was intended. Parents had a lot to say about who courted whom. They also had the power to prevent marriages which they judged to be undesirable.

Dating Games

Not many people would suggest we go back to the earlier forms of matchmaking. Free association between the sexes and free choice to marry, through an intelligent choice rooted in mutual love and compatibility, are a much more valid basis for a marriage. Yet our modern approach has its own problems.

For openers, some parents have the misguided idea that it is cute to have little children play at grownup dating and socializing. You can find dances even in the primary grades and proms at the junior high level. It may seem fun to the parents to use their children like dolls which they dress up in tuxedos and formal gowns. But it is rather pathetic in the kinds of emotional and psychological effects it can have on the children who are expected to go through these kinds of charades. It cheapens the whole boy-girl relationship and reduces it to a kind of game. Once the boy-girl relationship is experienced as a game, the real value, importance, and even fun of dating is lost in the shuffle. Our society reinforces the idea that dating is a game. We even have a popular TV show by that name.

Dating as a game can be rather vicious. It is especially cruel for the losers and those not invited to play. Singles bars are an end result of this tendency to reduce dating to a game in our society. The rules are complicated. Though the long-range object is marriage in some cases, the one-night-stand is the immediate goal. Losers go home alone.

In high school the dating game sometimes takes the form of a popularity contest or a numbers game. Who can date the largest number of "preferred" people? For some boys the object of the game is to "score." Even when they do not score, they sometimes will brag that they did. Otherwise they might appear to be losers.

The fact is that dating is a very valuable form of boy/girl relationship. This does not mean everyone should start dating as soon as possible and date as much as possible. Individual interest and inclination have an important role to play. Some people will date throughout high school. Fine. Some may not date on any regular basis until later. That's fine too. When we start dating and how much we date is not nearly so important as how we approach the dating relationship. Just how should we approach dating?

Happy Days—Sometimes

We have been saying all along that you are more than male or female genitalia. You are a male or female person with the task of integrating your sexuality into your total person and into your overall lifestyle.

We have also said that an important part of this development of your own identity and sense of self-worth depends on wholesome relationships with persons of the opposite sex. Men and women need each other for more than making babies. We need each other if each of us is to become a whole person.

Dating can play a very helpful role in this process. Dating is not the only way to achieve this kind of wholeness. There are other kinds of boy-girl relationships that can help, as we will see shortly. But dating is certainly a very good one.

Dating can and should be fun. It can provide companionship, laughs—an added dimension to everything from a football game to ice-skating or surfing. This is the surface benefit of dating. Underneath and in less conscious ways it can provide an ongoing education about yourself and about the mysterious opposite sex. It can help you mature precisely as a male or a female.

This does not mean every date must become a self-analysis exercise. The kinds of benefits we are talking about can take place quite naturally in the typical relationship—provided you approach dating as a friendship and not as a game.

To get a better idea of what is involved in the dating relationship for you in senior high, let's back up a bit. In the primary grades (ages 6-9) there is not much boy-girl relationship in the strict sense. Little children are aware that certain behavior is "proper" for them as either boys or girls. But beyond that, they do not make a big deal about it. Boys and girls can play together without any real awareness of being different.

By the middle grades there is a little more self-consciousness. Girls and boys tend to segregate when it comes to certain games and other activities. Boy-girl relationships are the giggly "Joe loves Mary" kind, and romance takes the form of grabbing someone's hat, pushing your romantic interest into a snow bank, or sending a secret note.

Once you hit puberty (when your genital sexual capacities emerge) around junior high, it is a different ball game. Boy-girl relationships tend to be a mixed bag. On the one hand, boys tend to group up, finding security in numbers. Girls do the same. Often boys and girls are just plain enemies. But on the other hand, there is a new curiosity about the opposite sex, a kind of undefined attraction.

Boy-girl activities, during the junior high years, are usually group activities. Any pairing off that does take place is usually "group imposed." The group decides that you like somebody or somebody likes you. You might even go through the external motions of a date, but the relationship is hardly what we are describing as an actual dating relationship. That takes more maturity than most junior high students will possess. Don't take this wrong. There is obviously a lot of pairing off that takes place in the junior high years. The alarming increase of pregnancies among girls under age 14 is concrete proof. It is also proof that junior high students are not mature enough to handle the responsibilities of an authentic dating relationship. It is too bad that society—including parents and peers—continues to pressure them into thinking that dating is both normal and desirable for them.

By the time people reach senior high, most are able to begin to benefit from the dating relationship. At the start there are many of the holdovers from the junior high years. Shyness, awkwardness, all kinds of embarrassing situations—they're part of the process. Unfortunately, there is no shortcut, no magic formula to apply so you can begin to feel at ease, self-possessed, confident in a dating situation. Despite all the advice an Ann Landers can give—and some of it is

good—it is a trial-and-error process. You make mistakes, do dumb things, say dumb things—or, just as bad, don't know what to say at all. There are times you wish a big hole would open up so you could crawl inside and hide. It is really not much comfort, but it is worth saying that just about everyone goes through the same awkward stage. So at least be reassured that you are normal, even when you do not feel that way.

Another normal experience is the heightened awareness and impulse of the specifically genital sex drive. Though this begins in puberty, it takes on more focus as we mature. This will not go away by any magic formula either. It will continue to play a part in any dating relationship we establish. How large a part it will play depends on us.

So the dating relationship involves some initial awkwardness. Along with that we also bring our genital sex drive to the relationship. There is one more important thing we bring to the relationship—and it is in fact the most critical at this point. We now bring to any dating relationship an expanded sense of our own person, something we did not have in junior high. We have a new awareness of our personhood, our uniqueness, our aloneness, our independence, and our responsibility for our own fate. This new awareness is fragile. It is untested. It is not

entirely clear. We pretty well knew the child of junior high years. We do not fully know this adult person inside us. Who am I really? More important, am I really lovable? worthwhile? okay? valuable?

Regardless of some unavoidable awkwardness and our often troublesome genital sex urges, those are the big questions we actually bring to the dating relationship. It is precisely through the dating relationship that you can often find the answers—if you view dating properly.

That is why being in love for the first time is so mind blowing. It seems no one ever really forgets that first love. What you discover for the *first time* in that first love are the answers. The new, more adult male or female ME is indeed lovable, worthwhile, okay, valuable. Just as I am!

But let's be clear about something. Being in love is different from having a crush or carrying on a fantasy relationship. Being in love is a two-way street. It means not only that we really love someone but also that the someone loves us back. A crush, on the other hand, is a one-way street. It is idolizing someone—like so many young teenagers idolize rock stars—and imagining what it might be like if that idol would choose one as his or her special person.

You see, in a crush or fantasy relationship the same questions and the same need to answer the questions are at work. We really do need to discover if we are lovable, worthwhile, of any true value to anyone. But a crush or fantasy relationship never gives us the answers. It is safe because we are never rejected. But in the end it is frustrating and has little real effect on growing up.

It is only in the real life relationships that we get the answers. Having a true love relationship for the first time is beautiful. Too often adults cheapen it by calling it puppy love or give advice like, "You'll get over it" or "It's just a phase you're going through."

Just be forewarned—if you have not experienced it already—that first loves do not usually endure. And breaking off or falling out of love is often painful, as the very words *break* and *fall* suggest. What makes it so painful is the feeling that we are being rejected—no longer lovable, valuable, worthwhile. Our new fragile adult ego is wounded.

For a few the wound is so deep that they may never really get over it, and they may not take the risk of loving again. For most, though, the wounds heal in time, dating resumes, and eventually a new love relationship is formed. Each of these love relationships reinforces our own sense of self-worth and each teaches us a little more about how to love in return. Through this process most people eventually become convinced of their own self-worth and master the capacity of selflessness involved in loving back. In this way we mature and are prepared to enter into the kind of permanent love relationship marriage and parenthood require.

So while dating should be fun, on the one hand, it is actually very serious business on the other. Dating has been very accurately called a school for adulthood and for marriage.

There is only one rule in this school: RESPECT THE PERSON YOU ARE DATING. We bring to the dating relationship certain needs to discover our self-worth, to be affirmed in our maleness or femaleness, to be valued as good even with our obvious weaknesses and faults, to be considered attractive not just physically but as a person. To the degree that we are still building up this kind of self-concept, we are very vulnerable. We can be easily hurt. We could be easily manipulated and used by others.

If any of this is true for you just now, it is equally true for those you date. They too need affirmation, acceptance. They too are in the process of forming their own sense of identity and self-worth. They too are vulnerable. You could easily hurt them, manipulate them, or use them for your own selfish interests.

In other words, you are to a real degree responsible for those you date. They are not things you use and then discard, totally ignoring their feelings or the fragility of their self-concepts. You can often inflict more serious wounds on a person by your words, your attitude, your manipulation than you could with fists or fingernails. It is in this context as much as in the context of the Sixth Commandment (which prohibits "adultery") that any discussion of the pros and cons of genital sex in a dating relationship must be viewed.

Boys whose primary objective in dating is "to score" may be satisfying their genital sexual urge. But it has a negative effect on their self-image. And it can be just as devastating to the girl who is used and treated as a kind of nonperson.

Girls who use sex as the bait to obtain dates and experience popularity fall into the same trap as the male makeout artists. In the long run they can only harm their self-concept. At the same time they are in fact using their dates to satisfy, if not their genital sexual urges, at least their ego needs. No matter how you slice it, dating that focuses primarily on genital sex is a "nobody wins" situation.

An idea as vague as one's self-concept does not have the dramatic impact of warnings about VD or pregnancy, but in terms of actual harm the psychological and moral wounds can in the long haul be much more serious. VD can usually be cured. An infant can be put up for adoption. But the deeply wounded self-concept may have to be endured throughout an entire adulthood and can ruin the chances for authentic, permanent love relationships. Think about that.

R-E-S-P-E-C-T Spells ...

We will come back to some more of the practical considerations about the right or wrong of non-marital sexual intercourse with a date in the next few chapters. In the meantime, if you just approach every dating relationship with a basic, sincere respect for the person you are dating, all dating relationships can be both fun and helpful to you and your date.

But the boy-girl relationships so important for you at this stage in your life are not limited to dating. If you are in a coed school, about half of your classmates will be of the opposite sex. How you relate in that kind of setting—in classes, in the cafeteria, at athletic and other extra-curricular events, in the halls, on the bus, by your locker—is just as important.

A putdown, an insulting remark, a snub, a smutty remark directed toward someone can wound and wound deeply. On the other hand, every smile, friendly greeting, offer of help, inquiry about how things are going can only help.

In other words, everyone should be included in your attitude of respect—even those you never have any intention of dating. Boys and girls need each other not just in the dating relationship. You need each other in the day-to-day give and take of ordinary life. It is all part of becoming a fully integrated man or woman.

Then there are special friends of the opposite sex. It may even be your brother or sister. It may be someone you work with at McDonald's, or someone in the band or on the school paper or in the student council. It may be a boy or girl who shares similar interests, a neighbor you grew up with, someone you can trust and talk with, but whom you have no real desire to date and vice versa. It may be the best friend of the person you are dating. It may be your best friend's current love. These kinds of friendships can be as valuable as the dating relationship in helping you to discover your self-worth and to become comfortable with your maleness or femaleness. If you have any friendships with persons of the opposite sex, cherish them. They are special gifts.

Close friends of your same sex also play a very important role in the process of forming your identity and integrating your sexuality into your person at this stage in your life. Often the one or two really close

friends you make during high school will remain true friends throughout your life.

For now such a close friend is someone with whom you feel really safe—someone who will not laugh at you and someone who can understand the troubles you might be having, especially in working out your dating relationships. Good friends are honest. They can tell you you are making a fool of yourself, but do it in a way that does not mean rejection. You can test out ideas and styles of behavior on a close friend and not be embarrassed. A friend picks you up when you are down. A close friend of the same sex is especially valuable when you go through a breakup with someone you have been dating seriously. They can reassure you that you are still okay even though your former love no longer seems interested in you. Obviously everyone would like to have such friends. Too often though we sit around waiting for someone to show up. There is only one sure way to ever find a friend like that. **Start being a friend to others.** Sooner or later somebody will return the gift!

Next ...

Up to now we have talked a lot about what being male or female should be like, what dating should be, what becoming an integrated person should be. Now we have to take a hard look at what is actually going on in the real world. It is not always a very pretty picture. Yet it is the only world we have, and it is the one we are forced to grow up in. So it is best to stay informed of what we are up against in trying to arrive at a mature, integrated sexuality. That's for the next chapter.

FOR REVIEW

1) Describe boy-girl relationships in the middle grades, in junior high, in senior high.
2) What are the key questions we bring to dating relationships?
3) Explain the difference between a crush and a love relationship.
4) What is the basic rule in dating? Explain it briefly.
5) Define: *chaperone, charade, manipulate.*

In consequence, God delivered them up in their lusts to unclean practices; they engaged in the mutual degradation of their bodies, these men who exchanged the truth of God for a lie and worshipped and served the creature rather than the Creator ... God therefore delivered them up to disgraceful passions ... They are filled with every kind of wickedness: maliciousness, greed, ill will, envy, murder, bickering, deceit, craftiness. They are gossips and slanderers, they hate God, are insolent, haughty, boastful, ingenious in their wrong doing ... One sees in them men without conscience, without loyalty, without affection, without pity (Romans 1:24-32).

6
What's Happening?

An aquarium can be all the world a fish might ever know. A confined fish has no way of imagining or discovering that marvelous ponds or lakes or oceans exist. Its aquarium is the only world, the whole world, for a fish. It does not know what it is missing out on.

We are all like fish in one sense: the only society we have ever personally experienced is the present one. So it is not too surprising that we take for granted that this society is "normal" or "natural" and that anything else is at least out-of-date if not plain unnatural.

For example, anyone born after 1965 takes for granted things like jet airplanes, television, and rocket flights to the moon and beyond. As a high school student, transistor radios, communication satellites, computers, and pollution have always been part of your world. Nuclear energy and nuclear weapons are also an integral part of the only world you have ever known. So are heart transplants and the polio vaccine.

We have one big advantage over the fish, however. Because of our intellect and access to history, we can escape the present and return to the past.

Unlike the fish, we have access to other times and other societies. We can compare and evaluate the present situation against

these. With this knowledge in our hands, we can then discover how to create a new future. We do not have to be prisoners of the only world we have ever experienced.

Reread the quote at the beginning of this chapter. It was written about two thousand years ago and describes the moral condition that existed at that time in a highly civilized society. If we were to change the writing style a little, we might think it was a speech delivered by some preacher last week. As was said earlier, our present society did not invent sex, sexual excess, or sexual perversion. They have been around as long as there has been history.

What is popularly being called the "sexual revolution" in our times is not a revolution if we measure it against the big picture of human history. It is a revolution only when we compare it to our society as it existed about twenty-five years ago. You were born after this "revolution." Since the only society you have experienced is this "post-revolution" society, it would be easy for you to imagine that this is the only possible and the most natural society. This is not so. But until you have something against which to compare our present society, it is going to be hard for you to evaluate our present sexual morals and behavior. That's the task of this chapter.

The Way It Was

To give us a framework, let's figure that as today's high school students you were born in the sixties, reached puberty, and began to form a more conscious awareness of society in the last few years. Your parents were born in the forties, reached puberty, and began to be conscious of their society in the fifties. Let's compare and contrast society in the fifties to that of the late seventies and on to the present. We will focus primarily on sexual attitudes and behavior, on what influenced them then and now.

One of the biggest changes that took place in that twenty-five-year period from 1955 to now took place in the area of media. TV is the most obvious example. But related to TV are all the other electronic inventions that have made it possible for us to be in almost instant touch with any part of the world.

You are, in fact, much more in touch with "what's happening" than your parents were when they were your age. Today you are drenched in media, both electronic and print.

The media has always had a tendency toward sensationalism, toward the bizarre, toward the out-of-the-ordinary. That's "news." It was "news" twenty-five years ago. But in our present media-drenched society this tendency can distort reality. If we constantly hear the sensational and seldom hear the ordinary, it is easy to begin to think the sensational **is** ordinary. Headlines scream: **40 ARRESTED AT A DRUG AND SEX ORGY.** They do not scream that the rest of the 100,000 people in the same town were at home with the family, at a friend's house playing cards, or at a basketball game. There are lots of reports like: "Pornography Now a Billion Dollar Business!" There are not too many news reports recalling that the Bible is still the all-time best seller. Today, then, it is much easier to get the impression that "everybody does it" and that sexual permissiveness is the norm. Hence, it is not seen as permissiveness.

There probably was, on the average, just about as much sexual permissiveness twenty-five years ago as today, but twenty-five years ago few people considered it the norm. It was considered license, a perversion, or abnormal—or even a sin. You will not hear too much talk about sin in today's media.

Sex sells. That has been an advertising principle as long as there has been advertising. But it has been perfected in your lifetime. Media lives by advertising. So media serves up a double dose of sex-oriented material. Not only does the news tend to overdose on sex-related stories. The advertising that pays for the media also uses sex as the basis of its ever-present suggestions about what we need to be happy.

Some of it is rather obvious and gross. An ad for spark plugs that has a picture of a well-endowed woman with a skimpy bikini is not too subtle. Some ads, typically those selling things like perfume or cars, have more class but the underlying message is the same: our product = sex = happiness.

Since this is the only society you have ever experienced, you probably do not even take much notice of these kinds of things. You tune them out, at least on the conscious level. But they are working on you unconsciously, subtly shaping your mind and behavior. While our minds are immensely more complex, sophisticated, and marvelous than any computer, they do share one trait with computers: if we put enough "garbage" in, we begin to get "garbage" out.

So a big difference between now and twenty-five years ago is that you are continuously and subconsciously bombarded by sex-oriented material in a way your parents never experienced. You are likely to think this situation is normal. Most parents and other adults are offended by it.

Sex is also a predominant theme in the entertainment world today. You cannot watch a professional football game on TV without being treated periodically to a leering shot of some scantily clad cheerleader (who is always female, by the way). Much of the lyrics of popular music today also has strong sexual overtones when it is not straight out

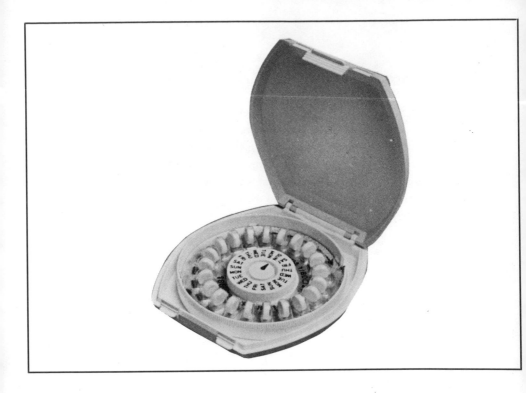

dealing with genital sexual acts. Most rock concerts have a heavily sex-oriented flavor in their entire production. Almost all the most popular sit-coms and dramas on TV do the same. Producers of movies actively seek an R rating, fearing that a PG or G will not attract the young people—who are the biggest patrons of movie theatres.

The fact is the media and entertainment fields have enveloped you in a sex-oriented world. Do you have any place to hide from these forces? Think about that. It was not always that way.

Probably one of the biggest influences on how present society views sex and sexual morality is the Pill. Twenty-five years ago a single girl's most common contraceptive device was the word no, motivated by religious conviction or by the fear of pregnancy. These motives tended to put restraint on most boys too. If contraception was practiced, it was largely the man's responsibility. He was in charge in that area if a couple had intercourse. The few birth control devices for women were either unreliable or beyond the reach of the unmarried girl.

The Pill is a truly revolutionary event in our times because both single and married women can now decide for themselves if they want to prevent pregnancy while they are sexually active. So a whole new generation of women has arisen. They are no longer forced—by the fear of pregnancy and the stigma of becoming an unwed mother—to avoid sexual intercourse. If a girl is going to remain virgin until marriage, she must now find some reasons other than fear for that choice.

Nobody knows for sure what choices are really being made. Some surveys indicate that less than 40 percent of women are virgin when they marry. Others reverse this, indicating that over 70 percent remain virgin until marriage.

One thing is sure. Given this new freedom, girls are under much more pressure to engage in non-marital sex in our society than was probably ever experienced by any generation of women until now. If you believed the "everybody does it" message of media and the entertainment world, it is easy to see how a girl might begin to feel abnormal for wishing to remain virgin until marriage—especially if it seems pregnancy need not be a risk.

Ironically, there are more unwed mothers today than at just about any time in our society's history—to say nothing of abortions. This, experts say, is due not only to promiscuity but also to ignorance about how conception and contraceptives like the Pill actually work. At best, for example, the Pill is not foolproof. If not taken according to schedule, it is virtually useless. Doctors say they have treated any number of young pregnant girls who had innocently thought that sneaking one of their mother's Pills a couple of times a month was all they needed.

Liberation

During the early sixties, before you were born, another kind of social revolution was also beginning. It had several dimensions, but they fed on each other and they all worked together to influence our many popular attitudes toward sex and sexuality today.

These dimensions can all be grouped under the general heading of "Liberation." Young people in the sixties sought liberation from the adult-controlled establishment—from its institutions, its hang-ups, and its hypocrisy. Women began in highly organized ways to seek liberation from the injustices imposed upon them by the centuries-old, male-dominated society. Authors, artists, and actors sought liberation from policies of censorship they felt were outdated, bigoted, and unconstitutional. Other minorities were equally active—Blacks, Hispanics, the elderly—seeking their own forms of liberation.

Encouraged by these other liberation movements, homosexuals and lesbians also began to fight openly for just treatment within our society. "Sexual preference is a private matter. It should not be used to discriminate in terms of jobs, police harassment, and the like." These arguments have been successful in the courts if not in changing popular attitudes.

Much of what these various movements of liberation have achieved in overcoming injustice, oppression, and discrimination deserves praise. Unfortunately, your age group began to become socially aware of these kinds of movements toward the tail end of their present momentum.

Often what you have been exposed to are the negative side effects of these movements rather than the good they have achieved. Much of what appears in the media today are the excesses and spinoffs. For example, you are probably too young to remember the first Woodstock Festival. It was a kind of music concert that celebrated the best aspects of the youth movement in the sixties: sincere interest in peace, harmony, fellowship, and a return to nature in the positive sense of that

expression. What you are more likely to view as a normal expression of young people's liberation from the establishment are the rock concerts today—some of which are barbaric, drug-stimulated riots. The scene not long ago of the mob of young people trampling its own to death in a rush for the best seats at a Cincinnati rock concert comes to mind. You can recall scenes of your own if you have been to a big rock concert.

Further, you cannot be expected to remember the inhuman treatment society regularly dealt out to homosexuals twenty-five years ago. So it is bound to be hard for you to fully appreciate the justice of most of the legal rights they have been able to achieve recently. You could easily fail to realize that equality before the law was the real issue. Today you could get the mistaken notion that homosexuality and bisexuality are as natural and normal as being heterosexual. The legal rights of the homosexual are one thing. The moral rightness or wrongness of being homosexual is another—and very complex—issue. We will get back to it later.

Undoubtedly the most horrendous side effect of these movements has been the legalization of abortion. Under the guise of a woman's legitimate claim to freedom over her body came the legal right for a woman to kill her unborn child. Even the legal father has no real right to stop her in most instances.

Strangely and sadly enough, abortion has become a "normal" option even for Catholic youth, although the Church has been in the forefront of the fight against it. Recently, a study of an East Coast abortion clinic turned up the curious fact that many of the clients were Catholic teenagers. More shocking was the fact that many of these teenagers felt that abortion was preferable to contraception in preventing the births of illegitimate children.

Almost as bad have been the side effects these liberation movements have had on the institutions of marriage and the family. Two out of every five marriages now end in divorce. (In some states it is two out of four and even slightly higher.) In the name of freedom, so some say, no one should be forced to stay married if he or she is dissatisfied—even temporarily. You also hear a lot about the very few married couples who opt for open marriages, mate-swapping arrangements, and such. Given the fact that marriage is now seen as a kind of "high risk" commitment, a few young people (about 4 percent) either opt for the trial marriage arrangement or simply agree to live together temporarily.

Another side effect of this fear of marriage is a whole new group of people in our society—the young singles. They simply put off plans for marriage indefinitely, but they do maintain an active sex life.

We could continue to list the bad side effects of the various liberation movements. For example, our current flood of hard-core pornography is an indirect result of certain legitimate battles against unjust censorship.

In all of this, the point remains the same. *Don't fall into the trap of presuming that since this is the only society you have experienced, many of its current sexual attitudes and practices are normal.*

Try to expand your vision, go back in history, consult with more than just the current media if you want to form a true idea of what human sexuality entails, what is normal, what is sick, what is wholesome, and what is sin. Otherwise your understanding will be too narrow and your behavior will often be limited to media suggestions. A "fish bowl," non-historical viewpoint will hurt your chances to become the fully human, sexually integrated person you are intended to be.

There is something else to consider too. Your parents and many of your teachers grew up in a radically different world. They came out of the fifties, were themselves quite possibly active in some of the liberation movements of the sixties and now view today's society from a much different angle than you.

Much of their judgment of what is good or bad, harmful or wholesome, normal or sick is formed out of an experience you have never had. On first glance, much of what they tell you might really seem out of touch with what is happening, something from "prehistoric" times. It might be worth a second look, though. No insult intended, but maybe it is you who are actually out of touch with what is really happening. Your view may in fact be one dimensional, shaped too much by what the media has been feeding you, focused on the bad side effects of some of the most just revolutionary movements in the history of our country (and of humanity). It may be that your ideas of what is normal are as narrowed as those of our friend the fish. Not being trapped as our fish is, you can check this out. And you can do something about it in terms of how you wish to spend your future.

Right On ...

A final note: words of sympathy and praise for you and your generation. The sex drive, being one of our strongest drives, has never been easy to control and to direct responsibly. It is doubtful that any generation of young people has ever had more pressures, more opportunities, or more excuses than yours to "go for the gusto" and forget about morality and responsibility. Though many adults may not tell you this, they admire the fact that so many of you have shown restraint and responsibility. Congratulations. And hang in there. Meanwhile, in the next chapter we will check out one of the most truly revolutionary views of human sexuality ever presented to us—the one given us by Jesus.

FOR REVIEW

1) In what sense is the *sexual revolution* not a real revolution?
2) Why is news in the media slanted to sensational or bizarre events?
3) If there was just as much sexual permissiveness twenty-five years ago as there is today, what is different regarding our values or attitudes?
4) Explain how the Pill created a real revolution in our times.
5) Name four of the liberation movements and explain their basic goals.
6) What percentage of young people choose trial marriages or decide to live together temporarily?
7) Define: *norm, liberation, harassment.*

> "Therefore a man leaves his father and his mother and cleaves to his wife, and they become one flesh. And the man and his wife were both naked, and were not ashamed" (Genesis 2:24-25).

7

The Rest of the Story

"startling ..." New York Times
"... extraordinary" Saturday Review
"thrilling ..." Chicago Tribune

These kinds of quotes are often found in the advertisement for a new movie or book. They give the impression that famous critics are praising the work; so it must be worth seeing or reading. But if you ever bother to actually read the reviews cited, you can sometimes find that the praise is lifted out of context and is not actually praise at all. For example:

"The only *startling* thing about this movie is the price of the admission, a real rip-off."

"The *extraordinary* stupidity of the plot is an insult to any intelligent reader."

"I found the most *thrilling* part of the movie to be its title. From that point on it went downhill quickly."

The same kind of "out of context" thinking frequently takes place when it comes to the Christian view of human sexuality and genital sexual activity. If we listened to some well-intentioned Christians, we

would get the impression that there is only one Commandment: the Sixth, which prohibits "adultery." We would also get the impression that sins against the Sixth Commandment are the worst we humans could commit. Just as often we could be led to think that our sexuality is a necessary evil, an unfortunate weakness we must tolerate in order to keep the race in existence.

That is why it is important to get the big picture, the rest of the story as it were, if we want to get a really accurate picture of human sexuality and human morality.

For example, primitive peoples thought various natural forces (sun, moon, wind, and such) were gods. They built their religious practices around efforts to gain the favor of these gods. It was rather common among these primitive peoples to worship fertility gods, forces who supposedly controlled the fruitfulness of their fields, their herds, and themselves.

They knew sexual intercourse had something to do with reproduction. They also knew it gave them a kind of "divine" pleasure. The logical next step was to conclude that sexual intercourse was a gift from a fertility god and that it must be pleasing to that god. To gain the god's favor, they would celebrate religious rites in which sexual intercourse

was a major part of the ceremony. Their view of sexuality came from their particular vision of humanity and nature.

On the other end of the spectrum, various philosophies in the past viewed everything as either matter or spirit. Whatever was spiritual came from a benevolent divinity. Whatever had to do with matter, including our bodies, came from an evil divinity. These divinities were at war with each other, and humans were caught in the middle, being both flesh and spirit. The goal for people who held this view was to become free from anything to do with matter and flesh so they could become united to the good divinity.

As you can imagine, this distorted view of reality influenced their attitude toward sex. Their view of human sexuality was very negative. At best it was a necessary evil. Some of the more devout male followers even suffered castration to free themselves from what they considered temptations of the evil divinity—meaning any sexual urges.

St. Augustine, a famous fifth-century Christian theologian, was influenced by this kind of philosophy before he became a Christian. Unfortunately, some of his negative attitudes toward human sexuality got mixed up with his otherwise excellent writing about Christianity.

Some of this negativism can still be found in certain schools of Christian theology today. Actually, much of the what is called "Puritanism" which influenced American thought about sex for several centuries can be traced at least indirectly back to Augustine. Some of it is still around and contributes to the distorted idea that Christianity and Christ are anti-sex.

So to understand what Jesus taught us about human sexuality, we must first form an idea of his overall vision of reality and of human nature. If we try to explain certain statements in the Gospel or particular teachings of the Church out of the context of this larger vision, they will seem as distorted as some of the older approaches to human sexuality.

Jesus Said ...

For starters, Jesus taught that all of creation—spiritual and material— comes from the Father and that it is good. So our bodies, including sexuality and our genital sexual capacities, are good.

Second—and this is a critical aspect of Jesus' vision—is the fact that each individual person is special to the Father and to himself. Each individual is personally loved as a child of the Father and called to everlasting happiness. This gives us our starting point for understanding who we humans are. Each of us, from the weakest to the strongest, the richest to the poorest, the ugliest to the most beautiful, is precious in the Father's eyes. Each of us has a unique dignity, a worth beyond imagination.

Because Jesus saw each individual human person in this light, he could give us the commandment, "Love each other the way you love yourself." We really should love ourselves, respect ourselves, recognize the dignity we possess as the Father's children—regardless of how we might appear by worldly standards of success or dignity.

Once we recognize our own dignity, it is not nearly so hard to recognize and admit that everyone else has his or her own special kind of dignity too, regardless of how they might appear to us superficially. They deserve to be loved the way we deserve to love ourselves. As a popular poster states: "God didn't make junk!"

Third, and this is very important too, Jesus teaches that the Father is a merciful, forgiving Father. We can mess ourselves up in a hundred ways that are not in keeping with the dignity and worth we possess as God's children. The Father will not interfere with our freedom to mess ourselves up. But neither will he withdraw his love for us. As soon as we get fed up with ourselves and try to get back on track, the Father will be there waiting with his forgiveness, his help, his love. The Father is not out to catch us in sin, as some imagine. He is out to grab us and hug us at the first sign that we want to turn from sin. That is part of the message of the parable of the Prodigal Son—the Father's continuing love and mercy for even the most ungrateful and stupid of us children.

But another message in that parable is just as important. We, unlike the older brother in the parable, must be as ready to forgive and forget the wrongs of our brothers and sisters as the Father is. Hidden in that parable is a footnote to the commandment to love one another as we love ourselves. It is this: "We should be as willing to forgive one another as the Father is willing to forgive each of us."

Building on this foundation of the Father's love and the personal worth of each of us as the Father's children, Jesus takes his vision of humanity one step further. He envisions us as a community, a fellowship, a family of mutual love, respect, justice, and active concern for one another. That's what our nature calls us to be, what we are intended to become, the goal the Father intends for us.

In this mixed-up world of selfishness, generosity, hatred, love, injustice, compassion, and violence you might be tempted to say such a vision is unrealistic, the dream of some romantic nut. But if you pause long enough to experience the deepest longings inside you, you will know that is really what you want too—and how it should be! Jesus' vision is not out of touch with reality. It just shows us how far from reality the human race often strays. This vision of humanity as a family—where mutual love, concern, justice, and respect are the norm—is often treated by Jesus under the symbol of the Kingdom. Jesus assures us this Kingdom will eventually come. So we can hope, no matter how bad things look right now. Jesus also tells his followers he expects them to do all in their own power to help build this Kingdom. Even the most insignificant and seemingly futile efforts in this regard are actually invaluable.

This brings us to one other important part of how Jesus looked at reality. Because everything created came from the Father, every-

thing created to some degree or other reflects or reveals to us something about the Father. The fancy way to say this is to say all creation has a *sacramental* quality.

Whenever we humans show love for one another or do some good deed for one another, our actions reveal a little bit of the Father's own love for us. Works of justice and acts of concern all reflect a little bit of the kind of Kingdom God is calling us to build. Just as important, each of these acts in fact helps bring that final state about. Our own good actions have a kind of **sacramental** quality. They reveal something of God and his love; they help perfect that Kingdom which is our human destiny.

It is only after we begin to form some idea of this *total vision* of Jesus about reality and human nature that we can begin to understand and appreciate the part of Jesus' teaching that deals specifically with our sexuality. It is only then that it will begin to make sense and not be seen as negative, warped, or anti-sex.

Male and/or Female Is Okay

Jesus taught that each person has a unique dignity and worth, and he considered a person's sexuality as an integral part of that dignity. As a result, he was anti-sexist, not anti-sex. That was a revolutionary stance within his male-dominated culture. As St. Paul phrased it, "You are neither male nor female, for you are all one in Christ Jesus." Jesus viewed and treated women as equals to men both in dignity and in their right to equal treatment within society. In his view gender could **never** be used as a basis for second-class citizenship.

Unfortunately some of his followers, swayed by the pressures and influences of their particular cultures, do still discriminate on the basis of sex. In practice there is still sexism within the Church, but it cannot be traced to either Jesus' words or his deeds. It is a defect in his followers.

Seeing our sexuality as an integral part of our human dignity and seeing that both male and female qualities are to be valued, Jesus in his own person displayed a wholesome integration of these qualities. He could be firm **and** gentle, affectionate **and** aggressive. He could focus all his attention on his goal, **and** he could give his total attention to the person who happened to be in front of him.

Comfortable with his own integrated sexuality, Jesus was at ease with both women and men, sought out both groups, and could publicly display an equal affection for men and women. He could deeply love the rough, smelly fisherman, Peter. He could also deeply love and show affection toward Lazarus' gentle sister, Mary. This ability and willingness to mingle with and show equal affection toward both men and women was a scandal to many of the people of his day. Pharisees openly criticized him for publicly associating with prostitutes, even reformed ones. Though there is no mention of it in the Gospels, it is not hard to imagine some of his enemies also accusing him of homosexuality because of his open affection toward his Apostles. Chances are he would face similar criticism in our own society today.

Operating out of his fundamental vision of our human dignity, Jesus considered human sexuality in its totality as good and as integral to our dignity.

Marriage Is for Keeps

When we get into the more specific area of genital sexual activity and behavior, we find Jesus' teaching has two levels to it. On the one level, he simply reaffirms and supports what reason can tell us about genital sex. On the second level, he is revolutionary.

First, he reaffirms that marriage should form a permanent bond between a man and woman. This is not a revolutionary part of his teaching. People had arrived at this conclusion long before him, just working from reason. Today, given our better understanding of biology, of evolution and of psychology, the arguments for marriage as a permanent bond can be made even more strongly.

We have already seen that from a biological point of view human mates must cooperate to *best* assure the survival and development of the offspring. This ongoing cooperation and shared responsibilities between mates which must extend over a period of years imply more than a casual or temporary relationship.

It must be granted that a single parent can achieve the task, provided there is some form of outside help from other family members, friends, or social agencies. In fact, single parent families make up about 25 percent of all families today—and the number is even higher in some parts of the country.

But this is still considered less than ideal in the context of our history and evolution. It is usually an outright disaster when the single parent is an unwed teenager, for example. Rearing a child means much more than providing food, clothing, and shelter. There is also a psychological dimension to the task. Again the most effective upbringing is seen to be that involving both a male and female parent figure, regardless of the sex of the child. Single parents readily admit that this is a much harder obstacle for them than providing the physical care required. Here especially a single parent must depend on persons of the opposite sex to help the child to achieve emotional and psychological balance.

In other words, it is generally agreed—above all by the single parents involved—that children are most effectively raised by a loving husband-wife team. Such a "team" implies some form of permanent commitment they make to one another before they decide to bring a child into the world.

In Jesus' time divorce was common and the approach was casual—much like today. He went against the grain and upheld the ideal of marriage as a permanent bond by quoting from an Old Testament tradition that went back centuries before him. He said, "For this reason a man shall leave his father and mother and cling to his wife and the two shall become one. Thus they are no longer two but one flesh" (Matthew 10:6). By referring to "no longer two but one flesh" Jesus was not referring to the obvious image of sexual intercourse, as many think. He was referring to the fruit of such a union, namely a child. The "one flesh" is a new person who comes literally from the two persons. So Jesus first sees the need for permanency to marriage in terms of the parenting which naturally flows from human mating. It is a position based on reason.

But Jesus, within his vision of things, also viewed human mating from a more revolutionary angle. He saw in the permanent commitment between a husband and wife and in their mutual love and support the potential for reflecting the Father's love. More than that, Jesus saw in the marriage relationship its potential as a school for love and an instrument for building up the Kingdom for which we are all destined. In other words, Jesus saw in marriage its potential *to be a sacrament*— promoting the Father's love on earth. That's revolutionary!

Clearly not all marriages are sacraments. That is not the point. What Jesus is telling his followers is that their marriage can be, should be such a sacrament. He calls and challenges those who accept his vision of reality to raise their natural mating and parenting to its full potential, to its most **fully human state,** to make of their marriage the sacrament it can be.

Once marriage is consciously viewed and freely entered into as a sacrament, divorce must be viewed as destructive of something holy, something God has put together and was called upon to witness. The seriousness with which Christians have traditionally viewed divorce can be fully understood when you understand the sacramental character of Christian marriage. Divorce in itself is viewed as sinful by the Church. Those are hard words. They can appear to be cruel, inhumane words, especially if your own parents have been divorced or if another family member or close friend is involved in a divorce. Yet judging the moral guilt in any particular divorce involves more than stating the moral principle regarding divorce. Applying the principle involves taking all of the important circumstances into account. More will be said about this in the next chapter.

It should be noted here, however, that what often appears to have been a sacramental marriage may never, in fact, have been one. For this reason the Church grants annulments in many cases. If the relationship had never really reached or had a chance to reach sacramental status, in the eyes of the Church no marriage ever existed. Both parties are free to marry if they wish.

For another thing, even in a sacramental marriage a couple can obtain a civil divorce and live apart. This certainly is not the ideal. It is not automatically immoral either. But in the eyes of the Church, the sacramental relationship, though wounded, is still binding. The parties are not free to marry a second time. That is the tough one! Some theologians today are seeking valid ways to enable such persons, in certain circumstances, to be allowed to remarry, even though the first marriage had been sacramental. It is a hotly debated topic, but it is doubtful we will see too much change in the Church's position in our lifetimes. The arguments against being allowed to destroy a sacramental marriage are strong and backed up by almost 2,000 years of tradition.

So not only does Jesus view human sexuality in general as

beautiful, good, and an integral part of our human dignity; Jesus also sees physical mating and parenting for what they ultimately can be—a true sacrament, a reflection and experience of the love and holiness of the Father.

Sex Is a Sacrament

It must be within this context that we seek to understand how Jesus viewed sexual intercourse and related acts. First of all, Jesus reaffirmed the position developed from reason over the centuries. On the purely biological level, the most obvious purpose for sexual intercourse is propagating the species. Since we have already seen that such propagating among humans involves some form of permanent bond between the mates, the natural forum for sexual intercourse is marriage.

The same conclusion can be found in psychology. Sexual intercourse involves a trust, a vulnerability, a self-giving, and a physical intimacy so total that some form of emotional and spiritual bond is implied.

It is obvious that people **can** engage in sexual intercourse as casually as they greet a friend with a kiss or a handshake. Prostitution, the one-night stand, and other forms of casual sex are as old as the human race. It is probably going on all around you among your peers. But humanity at the same time has always considered this kind of casual sex—lacking emotional and spiritual commitment—to be somewhat unnatural at best and at worst dreadful in terms of the unloved, unwanted babies that it brings into the world.

Jesus simply reaffirmed that gut feeling of humanity when he condemned adultery, fornication, and their variations. Outside the permanent commitment of marriage, sexual intercourse is less than nature intends it to be. In these circumstances, it is always **dehumanizing** to some degree. But once sexual intercourse is situated within its proper setting of a permanent emotional and spiritual commitment, Jesus once again gives us a revolutionary understanding. It is implied in his understanding of the potential sacramentality of marriage.

Sexual intercourse itself, being an integral part of the marriage relationship, has the potential to be a sacramental act. It can both express and deepen the mutual love, concern, and support implied in

the marriage commitment. In this way sexual intercourse itself can reveal God's love for us, help us experience that love, and enable us to better promote it among others. When sexual intercourse within marriage in fact achieves this sacramental quality, the physical act becomes all that it can be. And it helps us become fully human!

This can happen even though the married couple's only conscious focus is on the pleasure they are giving and receiving, and when they engage in sexual intercourse "just for the fun of it." It is still an acting out of their love and as such reflects the Father's love. Nothing dirty here. Nothing unwholesome, embarrassing, ugly, or unnatural. Within marriage as viewed by Jesus, sexual intercourse is a prayer, a sacrament—and fun.

Homosexuality

Much of what we have discussed can apply to the difficult issue of homosexuality. It is a difficult issue because we do not know what causes homosexuality. It might be an inherited trait; it might be due to a hormone imbalance; it might be brought about by family relationships we grew up with. Nor do we know whether homosexuality is a permanent condition or if it can be changed.

What we do know is that about one person in twenty is a homosexual. We also know that half of the men in America have had some kind of homosexual encounter in their lifetimes—as well as about 15 percent of the women. Besides that, we know that homosexuality is not contagious. In other words, we do not become homosexuals by knowing someone who is. Nor do isolated homosexual acts—sexual experiences with someone of the same sex—make us into homosexuals. Homosexuality appears to be an orientation—a fundamental viewpoint from which some people see sex and other people.

Given what we know of the Christian view of sexuality, there are several important things to be said about homosexuals.

1) Homosexuals are loved by God no less than heterosexuals.

2) Homosexuals have the same need to grow and to mature, to become whole people. They share equally in the challenge Jesus set for all of us: to become fully human, to accept all of the male and female traits within the human personality.

3) Homosexuals share the same need to express their sexuality—to relate to other people as male or female persons.

Until recently Christians have, in fact, been tough on homosexuals because they thought homosexuals were freely choosing to go against nature. Today, the Church's attitude is changing. While it teaches the ideal—that sex belongs in a permanent relationship committed to bringing life into the world—the Church also realizes that individuals are not guilty if circumstances make it impossible for them to attain that ideal. The Church does not approve of homosexual acts, but it reserves moral judgment to the individual and God.

If it happens over the period of the next few years that you discover you have a homosexual orientation, get good advice from someone who can help you to feel good about yourself. Be careful too that you are not jumping to conclusions. Confusion about their sexuality often leads people in their late teens to fear they are homosexual.

If you have that orientation, remember that you share with everyone else the same questions regarding human growth, personality, and sexuality. And remember too that everyone shares the same moral challenge—to become fully human. Homosexuals who have remained in touch with their faith and with the Church are helping other Christians to understand more about their orientation.

Okay, But ...

If we buy Jesus' total vision of reality, his view about human sexuality, marriage, and sexual intercourse makes all the sense in the world. If we do not buy that vision, all the arguments from reason and from religion will not do much good. In other words, before we can accept and begin to understand what Jesus teaches about human sexuality, we have to accept Jesus. Meanwhile, in the next chapter we will attempt to make some concrete and practical applications of what all this means for you. And since we really have not done so yet, we will have to get involved in the whole question of sexual morality or "When is it a sin?"

FOR REVIEW
1) How did earlier religions and philosophies sometimes view sexuality?
2) What are the major elements of Jesus' view of sexuality?
3) What is the Church's teaching regarding marriage?
4) Explain briefly what we know about homosexuality, given the Christian perspective.
5) Define: *sacramental, sexism, fornication.*

At daybreak he reappeared in the temple area; and when the people started coming to him, he sat down and began to teach them. The scribes and the Pharisees led a woman forward who had been caught in adultery. They made her stand there in front of everyone. "Teacher," they said to him, "this woman has been caught in the act of adultery. In the law, Moses ordered such women to be stoned. What do you have to say about the case?" (They were posing this question to trap him, so that they could have something to accuse him of.) Jesus bent down and started tracing on the ground with his finger. When they persisted in their questioning, he straightened up and said to them, "Let the man among you who has no sin be the first to cast a stone at her." A second time he bent down and wrote on the ground. Then the audience drifted away one by one, beginning with the elders. This left him alone with the woman, who continued to stand there before him. Jesus finally straightened up and said to her, "Woman, where did they all disappear to? Has no one condemned you?" "No one, sir," she answered. Jesus said, "Nor do I condemn you. You may go. But from now on, avoid this sin" (John 8:2-11).

8
But Is It a Sin?

Let's jump right into it this time. The little paragraph that follows is a brief but rather complete summary of the Christian moral principles dealing with genital sexual behavior. These principles flow from that vision of Jesus we discussed in the last chapter.

Genital sexual activity (sexual intercourse and those proximate actions which lead to it) finds its most perfect and fully human expression only between a woman and a man bound together in a mutual love publicly expressed in the permanent commitment of marriage. Any genital sexual activity outside that relationship is at the minimum morally suspect because it violates a moral principle.

That pretty much says it all. Please read it over a few times. Note at once that we are not yet in the question of "Is it a sin?" Sin is a tricky thing. It involves personal **freedom** of choice, the **knowledge** one possesses, the **motives** one has, and all the **circumstances** that color one's freedom, knowledge, and motives.

Being guilty of sin is a very personal matter and is ultimately a

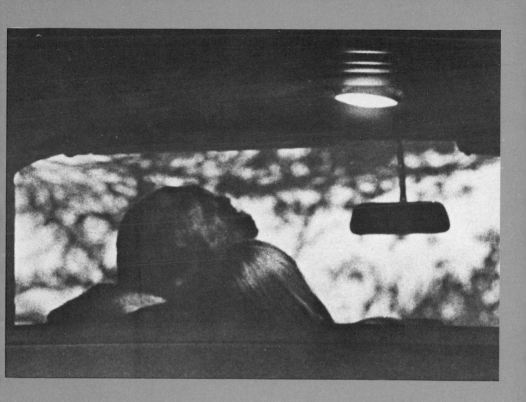

matter that is settled between God and the individual. Here we are just talking about morality in terms of the nature and role of our human sexuality in the overall picture of our humanness. Genital sex finds its most human expression within marriage. Outside marriage, genital sex is at the minimum something less than it is supposed to be. Rape, adultery, prostitution, non-marital intercourse (even when the couple is in love), mutual or solitary masturbation, genital sexual relationships between homosexuals or lesbians—all of these must at the minimum be judged as less than fully human and some can be considered terribly dehumanizing. It is hard to imagine, for example, when rape does not injure both the victim and the rapist—physically, psychologically, emotionally, and spiritually.

On the other hand, things like exhibitionism, voyeurism, sadomasochism and similar behavior usually flow from psychological sicknesses that just happen to find expression in the area of sexual behavior.

Putting this back into perspective, the basic moral challenge that Jesus always presents to us is *to become fully human on all levels.* This includes the dimension of our sexuality and sexual behavior, but there is much more. A person can be as pure as the driven snow when

it comes to sexual behavior and still be a warped human being. There is more to being fully human than keeping our sex life in order. A vowed celibate twisted by hypocrisy, greed, or prejudice is missing the point just as much as or maybe more so than the adulterer. Recall the story of the woman taken in adultery at the opening of this chapter.

Jesus did not consider "sex" the big sin. He considered the big sin to be our decision to dehumanize ourselves or someone else. What form our refusal to become fully human takes is rather unimportant if in the long haul the final result will be the same. Yet once you begin to see your dignity as a beloved child of God and see just how beautiful, holy, and sacramental the fully human **use** of your genital sexual powers can be, you can appreciate just how dehumanizing the **misuse** of those same powers can be.

Further, if that misuse means, at the same time, using another child of God just for your own kicks, the dehumanizing effect is even more depressing. Some people can get more upset about litter in a public park than they can about dehumanizing themselves and others by using their sexual capacities as if they were the toys described earlier by the visitor from outer space. Those people have a rather distorted view of things. Many people would be horrified if they heard that some barbarian types used the pages of the Bible to wrap garbage. Yet some of these same people might think nothing of expecting their date for the night to allow them to use his or her body as a plaything. Seeing the barbarian's act as scandalous and failing to see the real immorality of their own actions is also a distortion of human reality.

So there is actually nothing obscure about Jesus' moral teaching regarding genital sex. He sees us as children of God. He calls us to

achieve our full potential, to become fully human. Then he challenges us to act that way. Anything less only tends to warp our humanness. This will not make sense to people who never look beyond their genitals, or who fail to recognize the dignity they possess as human beings. But for those caught up in the vision and the challenge Jesus offers us, his teaching on sexuality makes all the sense in the world.

This does not mean Jesus' teaching is always easy to follow. It does not mean a person will not fail sometimes. But knowing who we are, what we are called to be, and what the real nature of sexuality is is 90 percent of the battle. Without such an awareness of the beauty and full potential of our sexuality, we can only hope to bump along blindly. Lacking such a vision, our sexual urges and drives will often end up leading us, enslaving us, and dehumanizing us. Lacking such a vision (and the education it implies), genital drives and urges will be experienced as a bothersome duty, a bewildering force, a casual plaything, or a powerful weapon for manipulating persons.

Those four experiences just mentioned—duty, bewildering force, casual plaything, weapon for controlling others—represent the major viewpoints we have for understanding sexuality if we have trouble accepting the vision of Jesus. Each viewpoint has its own prophets, high priests, theologians, and faithful in history and in today's society.

So if you have a sincere argument against Jesus' view—and not just one based on a whim, on a fear of challenge, or on a surrender to peer pressure—you owe it to yourself to check out other possible explanations of what to do with your sexuality, your future, your very existence.

Jesus and all sincere followers of Jesus will not try to force Jesus' vision on you. The decision must be your own. Just do not reject the Christian view of sexuality and its moral principles until you know what you are rejecting—and until you find something better to replace it. It would be useful to keep in mind that, regarding its moral principles, the Church doesn't declare something harmful because it is wrong; on the contrary, the Church warns us that something is wrong because it is possibly harmful.

No Need for Lawyers

But is it a sin? As we said earlier, sin is a tricky thing. Any act or failure to act that results in dehumanizing you, or making you less than you can be, is called **immoral** or **sinful in principle.** Things like the Ten Commandments, the Church's official teaching on matters like divorce, birth control, social justice, and attending Mass on Sunday are statements of such moral principles. When some action or omission by its very nature contradicts what it actually means to be human, it is **sinful in principle.**

But when you get in the area of *personal sin, personal responsibility,* and *personal moral guilt,* it is a whole new ball game. A person kills another. Clearly a moral principle has been violated and a less than perfectly human result followed. (Obviously, in terms of human nature, it is more human to be alive than it is to be dead.)

But can we call the person who did the act a murderer, implying personal moral guilt and responsibility for this dehumanizing result? Not until we get all the facts involved in determining moral guilt. And it is virtually impossible for us to get all of these. Only that person and God can know for sure. Before we can tag a person with moral guilt and the title "sinner," we have to check out some important things. Did the person act freely, uninfluenced by some external force or inner compulsion that takes away or weakens freedom? What were the person's motives? Did the person want to kill or was he or she being careless? Did the person feel that some condition like self-defense was involved? What were the circumstances? Did the killing take place on a field of battle? in a barroom brawl? in the act of defending one's property from a burglar? while driving home in a drunken or otherwise spaced-out state?

Even when guilt *is* present, how we answer these questions can determine what can be called *degrees of guilt.* A drunk who kills a person in an accident is normally guilty of what courts call manslaughter. A hit man who assassinates someone for pay is guilty of what the courts call first degree murder. Both people are guilty because killing always violates a moral principle. But the guilt is obviously greater in the second instance.

So assessing the moral guilt or the sinfulness of an individual person, be it someone else or yourself, involves much more than agreeing that a particular moral principle was violated. A prostitute, for instance, clearly is in violation of a moral principle. She—or he—might be far less guilty, however, than the person who buys the service, the pimp who profits from it, or the cop who accepts graft to look the other way. A young couple who live together outside marriage are also violating a moral principle. But personal sinfulness might not be as great as it appears at first. They may have the misguided idea that such a trial arrangement is the best way to arrive at the decision to marry. The motive is good, the goal is praiseworthy. Their information is what is actually wrong. Such a live-in arrangement seldom works out in reality. But whatever dehumanizing effects result, they are not nearly so bad in most cases as those which result when a young man or woman goes in for casual sex and sleeping around.

Masturbation is a less than fully human use of one's genital sexual capacities. In principle, then, it must be labeled sinful. Determining for ourselves whether we are personally guilty and determining just how sinful it is for us is another question. Myths generated from the past would have us believe that masturbation can cause blindness, sterility, insanity, acne, growth of hair on the palms, or balding of the scalp. If it did, in fact, have some of those more horrifying

effects, it would have to be judged as very dehumanizing and therefore very sinful in principle.

Since it has none of those kinds of effects, it is no longer regarded as the horrible sin it has been considered formerly. But it is still considered sinful in principle. So masturbation, like other forms of sexual immorality, must be viewed in terms of **all the concrete circumstances** to ultimately determine the seriousness and degree of personal guilt or sinfulness.

Most moral theologians and most priests in the Reconciliation room today agree that masturbation by adolescents, while a violation of a moral principle, rarely involves serious personal guilt.

Masturbation is something to discuss openly and frankly with a priest or other suitable advisor. It is not a matter for panic. It does not have to be all that embarrassing either. It may not be matter for serious personal guilt, but it is still a violation of a moral principle. It is being less than fully human. We should never be willing to settle for that, especially if we appreciate our inherited dignity as God's own.

Visions or Garbage?

What about sexual fantasies? The moral principle involved is this: wanting wholeheartedly to do something immoral—even if we cannot carry out the act—tends to have some of the same dehumanizing effects. This follows along the lines of the "garbage in—garbage out" principle we mentioned earlier.

On the positive side, fantasy is a part of being human, and people fantasize all the time. It is a natural and creative use of our imaginations. In fact, the best and biggest choices in our lives are always accompanied by hopeful planning and bright dreams.

On the other hand, the TV programs that people call "garbage" are examples of useless fantasies. They often show characters falling in love literally in 9 or 10 minutes. The couple know nothing about each other—not their pasts, their future plans, their present hopes or fears. They never discuss their concerns about pregnancy, birth control, or venereal disease. And yet things rarely go wrong, or if they do, somehow the problem is corrected within the hour (she was not really pregnant).

The point is that if our sexual fantasies demonstrate no more imagination than TV "jiggly" shows, they are also garbage. So really lusting after some girl or boy in your class, spending a lot of time "programming" your imagination with "jiggly" fantasies, and refusing to consider any of the natural concerns or consequences are ways of treating that other person irresponsibly.

Did you ever have a vivid dream in which a friend of yours played a major role, say as a villain who treated you very badly? Did you notice how, when you met that person the next day, your first reaction was to begin to relate to your friend as you experienced him or her in the dream? It is kind of spooky.

The same psychological law is at work in understanding the potentially dehumanizing nature of sexual fantasies. They can affect how you relate to the people involved. And that means they can also affect your behavior and shape your own identity.

We are talking, of course, about **fantasies that we plan and then work at,** that we spend a lot of time elaborating and lingering over. We are not talking about all the fantasies that will just jump into our heads, and that we do not take all that seriously. Many times boys have erotic dreams, for instance, which accompany **nocturnal emissions,** sometimes called **wet dreams.** These are naturally occurring events which a boy need not be embarrassed or concerned about.

Pornography is much the same as fantasy and the same principles apply. Pornography is basically a "fantasy aid." Checking out the latest slick magazine sitting on a newsstand is one thing. Habitually getting kicks by pondering pornographic material and dwelling on the fantasies it helps stimulate is something else.

So dwelling on sexual fantasy and pornography, as we are describing it, is in principle immoral. Willingly and frequently indulged in, it can be considered sinful. If it has become a repeated habit for you, confront this defect honestly in yourself—in much the same way and for the same reasons you should confront patterns of masturbation you may have developed. If possible, ask some adult you trust about your concerns. At this point in your life, it is just as likely that you may be too critical as it is that you may be dishonest with yourself. Do yourself a favor: get good advice.

What Does "It" Mean When You "Do It"?

Non-marital sexual intercourse—that is, any sex outside of marriage—is a less than fully human use of our genital sexual capacities. In terms of moral principles it is immoral, period. On this level of moral principle, it always falls short of the dignity and fully human behavior of which we are capable, and to which we are called. It is a misuse of our genital sexual capacities. On the level of moral principle, it is seriously sinful.

If we want to be honest about the moral question of non-marital sex and with the real issue of our call to become fully human, sexually whole persons, we should start on this level of moral principle. Non-marital sex is less than fully human. It is sinful in principle. It dehumanizes us. Since there must be a partner, it also has a dehumanizing effect on him or her.

A judgment of personal moral guilt and the dehumanizing effects will depend, as in applying all other moral principles, on the concrete circumstances involved. Forcible rape of an eight-year-old is perhaps the worst form that sexual intercourse can take. Psychologically achieved rape of a date by means of seduction and a manipulation of her or his emotional needs is also a form it can take. Getting carried away by our passions when we honestly had not planned to is another. Cruising and finding a "pick-up" is still another. In a sense, no two situations are quite alike. There will always be variations in terms of free will, motive, conscious awareness, and the partner involved.

Americans, you may not be aware, avoid touching as often as possible compared to people in many other cultures. Men especially are afraid of being labeled homosexual or effeminate if they touch one another. Yet, from birth on, we need to be touched and to touch others. And touching is a powerful way to communicate our feelings of friendship, love, and sexuality. Because we, as Americans, do not usually touch others except as a warm-up to sex, we often mistake touching meant as a loving gesture with touching as a sexual gesture: "She touched me. She must want sex." **As a result of our "touch deprivation," we are also open to overwhelming feelings of love or sexual arousal or both when we do get hugged or touched.** Thus we even mistake touching meant only as a sexual gesture with touching as a loving gesture: "He touched me. He must love me."

Furthermore, as teenagers we experience the loss of touch as a loving gesture because oftentimes parents are embarrassed to touch teenagers once they have reached puberty. What parents are reacting to is the **incest taboo** which forbids sexual intercourse between members of a family. Parents often worry about their feelings of admiration for their teenagers' adult, attractive bodies.

We need daily activities to help satisfy our hunger for touching—a hunger as real as our hunger for food. Dancing, sports, hospital or nursing home jobs — all of these activities on a daily basis will help satisfy the need to touch and be touched.

Only you and God can ultimately determine how sinful and de-humanizing a particular act of non-marital sexual intercourse might be for you. But don't play games with your life or someone else's. Sex is too important. Don't try to convince yourself and/or your partner that "It's okay for us, because we love each other," or "It's okay because everyone else does it," or "It's okay because she (I) can't get pregnant now," or "It's okay because we'll never see each other again anyway and no one is going to get hurt," or "It's okay because we plan to marry someday." It is never okay: it is always something less than a truly human use of your genital sexual capacities. It is always less than a fully

human, loving, honest relationship with another of God's own. The essential question is "Why not the best?" Why not make sex all that it should be? Why should you settle for less?

Let's Get Practical

There is a good chance you are in at least general agreement that a casual, irresponsible approach to non-marital sex is wrong. You might be in general agreement too that "waiting until marriage" is at least a worthy ideal.

But just what do you do until the preacher comes? Given the strength and urgency of the genital sexual drive, and given the fact that you are involved in dating, how do you keep sexual matters in control? You may have questions like "Just how far can we go and still be doing the right thing?" We will give those questions a shot in the next chapter.

FOR REVIEW
1) Rewrite into your own words the summary statement of the Christian view regarding sex.

2) Other than the Christian view, what are the other four major viewpoints regarding sex?
3) Explain briefly the concept of *degrees of guilt*.
4) Why is masturbation wrong in principle?
5) Explain the *garbage in—garbage out* principle with regard to sexual fantasies.
6) Define: *rape, voyeurism*.

"Which commandment is the first of all?" Jesus answered, "The first is, 'Hear, O Israel: The Lord Our God, the Lord is one; and you shall love the Lord your God with all your heart, and with all your soul, and with all your mind, and with all your strength.' The second is this, 'You shall love your neighbor as yourself.' There is no other commandment greater than these" (Mark 12:28-31).

9

Waiting for the Preacher

Here's a quiz to check out your common sense.

INSTRUCTIONS:

You are a healthy, red-blooded young person in senior high school. You enjoy dating and are about as successful as anyone else when it comes to dating.

In one important area you are not too sure just how much your own attitudes are like those of your peers. But you, at least, are convinced that non-marital intercourse and some of the other kinds of heavy, orgasm-producing fooling around on a date are immoral, unfair to your date, and too risky to get into. You are deeply determined to avoid it. You get the urges all right. Sometimes they are really strong. You are definitely interested, in other words, but you are convinced you should not go that route. In order to stand by your convictions and to avoid creating more problems with arousal and self-control than you already have, which choices below would be the *common sense* choices?

These are for boys:
  1) If you are taking your date to a movie but there is nothing special showing, would you choose the one at the drive-in or the one at a regular theater?

2) Your date's parents are not home when you arrive; in fact, they are going to be gone for the evening. Do you suggest staying there and watching TV or going out somewhere, like bowling, skating— or at least for a walk, if money is a problem?

3) You are turned on before you even leave the house, and you are taking this really cute girl to a party. There will be free access to beer, liquor, marijuana, or whatever. Do you begin using drugs and encourage your date to do the same or do you hold back?

4) You are parked after a date and are doing some routine kissing. You like the girl, but you are not getting worked up. You are still within your range of control. To your surprise your date begins to get worked up, starts kissing you back with real passion, some heavy breathing and all. Do you keep making out or do you suggest it is time to be getting home?

5) You have been dating this girl for some time and you are both serious. You honestly love each other. Lately, you have been spending more and more time alone and just making out on dates, rather than doing sports things, going to parties, double dating, etc. The last few dates have gotten close to the point of no return and you both know it. Do you:
   a) Get some condoms to keep with you—just in case?
   b) Break off with the girl?
   c) Have a frank talk with her, tell her your desire to avoid inter-course, explain how worked up you have been getting, and then work out some rules together for cooling it?
   d) Have another idea? Explain.

These are for girls:
   6) You have a date to go to a beach party with a guy you really like. You know there is eventually going to be some making out before it is all over. That is okay with you. You also have a rather cute figure, being well-endowed in the right places. Do you wear a string bikini or something that gives you a little more material for your money?

   7) A nice looking, popular boy finally gets around to asking you for a date. The word is out among your friends that he's something of a

makeout artist, but you are not sure if it is just gossip or not. He shows up with a van equipped like a rolling bedroom and suggests going to a drive-in movie. Do you say "okay" or do you suggest a theater or other activity that is a little more public?

8) You are doing some routine kissing with a guy you have dated a lot and are beginning to like a lot. For the first time since you have been dating he starts moving his hands toward places where you are not suntanned. It is obvious he is getting worked up. Do you:
   a) Slap his face and scream?
   b) Keep on kissing but keep pushing his hands away?
   c) Politely but firmly say it is time to stop making out and start heading home?

9) Your parents are going away for the weekend and you are left to baby-sit your younger brother. Do you invite your steady over alone to watch TV together, or do you invite several friends, including your steady?
   Also, do you have your friends wait in the car while you two say good night or do you send them home first so you can take more time saying good night?

10) You have been dating this boy for some time and you are both serious. You really love each other. Lately, you have been spending more and more time alone and just making out on dates, rather than doing sports things, going to parties, double dating. The last few scenes have gotten rather close to the point of no return and you both know it. Do you:
   a) Start using some contraceptive—just in case?
   b) Break off with the boy?
   c) Have a frank talk with him, tell him your desire to avoid intercourse, explain how worked up you have been getting, and then work out some rules together for cooling it?
   d) Have another idea? Explain.

This is for both boys and girls:
11) Both you and your regular date agree that you do not want to start having intercourse. But can you agree that it is okay to touch one another's genitals sometimes when you are kissing? Yes or no?

Good News and Bad News

We told you this was a quiz to check out your common sense. The answers should be obvious to a person who is determined to avoid non-marital sex. We did not say such an approach makes you popular. By some people's standards the common sense answers would seem downright stupid.

The point in all this is that you already know what is sexually stimulating to you. Through experience and/or through a course like this you have a pretty good idea what is going to be sexually stimulating to the girl or boy you are dating. You know some situations are clearly high-risk situations for any sexually normal person.

So there is no new trick to avoiding non-marital sex today that was not around fifty years ago. It is just a matter of common sense, looking ahead, making some plans, taking some precautions, avoiding the obviously high-risk situations, stopping while you still can. It is still a matter of being frank, open, up-front with your friend when a relationship gets serious and heavy. Once love is involved, the biological attraction for intercourse takes on a new kind of urgency. Emotions, the desire to please, to express what you feel in your heart—all of that is real and good. When love is involved, you have to take even more pre-

cautions, be more careful of the high-risk situations. And you have to talk it over so you both become more sensitive to whatever problems of control the other might be having. It can be done. It has been done by millions of people for centuries. The urgency of your genital sexual drives is not any stronger than that of your ancestors. Your feelings of love are not either. The common sense solutions have not changed over the centuries and they still work.

Today, there **are** two reasons why it might be harder for you than for your ancesters to avoid non-marital sex and still maintain a life of dating, including falling in love.

We have talked about one of them already. It is the fact that arriving at the decision—the actual determination to avoid non-marital sex—is much more difficult today. It's not a popular decision today. People often are laughed at for making it. It is a revolutionary decision; it is a decision of a counterculture—as radical as the decision some youth made in the sixties to go to jail rather than fight in what they considered an unjust war. They opposed public opinion and a powerful establish-ment. They had to pay a price. Their motive? They preferred jail rather than being untrue to themselves and their deepest convictions.

That's the catch. The decision to avoid non-marital sex, to go against the current "establishment" among your peers and in large segments of adult society requires conviction. Ultimately it must be rooted in motives stronger than fear. This kind of conviction and the resulting courage to pay the price must be rooted in the kind of religious faith we have been discussing throughout this course.

The powerful helps that faith provide are prayer and grace. In prayer we listen for God within ourselves and ask him for the strength to make the right decisions. And in listening and asking we also hear a lot about our deepest needs and our real feelings. A moment's prayer can summon up genuine compassion for the other person, wisdom regard-ing our real motives, and maybe even humor—being able to laugh at foolish situations we get ourselves into can be the shortest way out of them.

The second problem you have that your ancestors did not have is a much greater degree of freedom from adult supervision. It may not seem that way to you. You have curfews, the restriction on where you can go, and the endless questions both before and after a date. To say nothing of the lectures, warnings, and threats like "If ever I hear that you . . ."

It may seem a real bummer, but if your parents are doing any of that, you are actually lucky. The fact is, even when parents are very concerned and are trying to "protect" you, you have freedoms today that simply did not exist twenty-five or fifty years ago among high school students. Access to wheels is one. So is your access to booze and other drugs. Unless you live in a really small town, there are plenty of places you can go with your friends (or your friend) to avoid adult eyes. And, sad to say, some parents just do not care what their kids do.

Petting, Emergencies, Morality

We passed over a couple things in that little quiz. Both need a bit more comment. The first is petting. To be sure we are talking about the same thing, let's define it here as touching, caressing, or in other ways stimulating the primary sex organs, including the female breasts. Petting can involve either direct contact or indirect contact through clothing.

Such activity normally has the effect of arousing the persons involved for sexual intercourse and orgasm. Even when this is not the intention of the persons involved, petting still tends to have that effect. Hence, in principle petting is considered immoral for unmarried persons.

Given the nature of the act, given the overall idea that genital sex belongs in marriage, it should be plain enough why petting is wrong in principle. However, for two people in love, especially if they are sincere about not wanting to have sexual intercourse, petting might seem a alternative expression of their affection and their physical feelings. The problem is that petting itself is a big step toward intercourse. It is like throwing gas on a fire you already have trouble controlling. So just from a common sense point of view—if you are determined to avoid non-marital intercourse—petting is a bad idea.

A second matter only referred to in the quiz was the idea of contraceptives as a precaution—just in case you get carried away. This is much tougher. Parents of adolescent girls today agonize over that one. Even the best of us can have a weak moment. Just one time is enough for pregnancy and maybe a ruined future. So why shouldn't parents let their daughter go on the Pill or get fitted with one of the devices available today? It seems logical enough.

But, they then argue with themselves, "If we do that, won't she think we condone non-marital sex when in fact we are opposed?" "Will she think we are actually encouraging her? Or at a minimum will she become less guarded, more willing to take chances, knowing that if she and her date do get carried away it will at least be safe?" This kind of dilemma did not exist twenty-five years ago. It is very real today.

Just how would you decide if you were a parent today and you had a daughter your age? Take a few minutes now to think it over. In line with these questions, here are a few additional facts.

Apart from not being totally foolproof, the **Pill** has many potentially bad side effects (blood clots, etc.), especially for girls in their teens. It is medically risky and should **never** be used without a doctor's ongoing supervision.

The **IUD** (intrauterine device) is a small wire coil that must be placed within the uterus by a doctor. It also does not have a good track record in terms of medical risks and it has been known to slip out undetected. Moreover, it is probably an abortifacient—that is, the IUD does not prevent conception, rather it causes the abortion of a newly-conceived human being when the fertilized egg tries to implant itself in the womb. In other words, the evidence indicates that it kills newly-conceived babies.

The **diaphragm,** a device that fits over the entrance to the uterus to prevent sperm from reaching the ovum, does work. It must be initially fitted by a doctor, however, and it must be put in place by the girl shortly before intercourse. It is not very practical if its purpose is to help someone who has been "taken by surprise." It is more for someone who is planning to be sexually active.

There are also **foams** that kill sperm within the vagina, but these must be used rather soon before intercourse. They are not considered a highly reliable contraceptive method.

Don't get this wrong. Any of the above contraceptives do work in the majority of cases. And there are others. But each has its own set of drawbacks, to say nothing of the moral principles involved in using them.

But to get back to the question. Would you provide your teenage daughter, whom you basically trust and consider to be a moral person, with some form of contraceptive—just in case? Tough, isn't it?

For the boys reading this, be grateful that you cannot become pregnant. And for God's sake (that's a prayer, not a vulgarism), never forget the awesome power you have to make a girl pregnant. We do not recommend that you carry **condoms** in your wallet any more than we recommend that the girls start taking the Pill—even though condoms are not nearly as complicated. That does not make it any less a moral question.

Would you suggest that your own teenage son keep condoms with him? What do you think the effect might be on his attitude toward intercourse? on his behavior?

In any event, here are a few facts for you, so you are not misinformed. Condoms are the best method, other than abstinence, for preventing the spread of VD. Condoms are not foolproof; some are defective when they come from the factory and some break or slip off during intercourse. Since they have to be put on carefully, it is generally safe to say that if someone can take the time to put one on, he has enough time to regain control of the situation. Usually they are part of the game plan. Also, a condom carried around in the wallet for more than a year is a high-risk contraceptive because it is much more likely to be or to become defective.

Back to the question. Should a boy or girl who personally has no intention of having sexual intercourse until marriage take some precautions ahead of time—just in case things should ever get out of control?

We won't answer that one for you because we cannot answer that one for you. All we can say is that it is a moral question, and that you should seek moral counsel from a priest, counselor, and/or your own parents if you are considering taking some precautions.

This kind of nitty gritty discussion is necessary. There is too much at stake in terms of human life, your future, the future of the boys or girls you are dating, to gloss over some of these realities.

FOR REVIEW

1) What are two reasons why it might be harder for you to avoid non-marital sex than it was for your ancestors?
2) What is the worst risk you face regarding sexual matters?
3) What are the types of contraceptive techniques? Explain each briefly.

Jesus said to them: "The children of this age marry and are given in marriage, but those judged worthy of a place in the age to come and of resurrection from the dead do not. They become like angels and are no longer liable to death. Sons of the resurrection, they are sons of God" (Luke 20:34-36).

10

Until Death—and Beyond

They gather every Saturday night dressed to the hilt. Party dresses, fancy suits, great hairdos, jewelry, and aftershave abound. There are lots of giggles and gossip about who's going with whom. Rumors of budding romances are in the air. So is music, a lively four-piece band that plays almost non-stop for three hours.

The event? A weekly dance at a senior citizen center outside St. Louis. The scene is duplicated in towns and cities throughout the country each week. Average age of those attending is 73. Except for the gray hair and some creaky joints, you would think you were at a high school dance. Not infrequently there is a wedding to celebrate, the result of one of the budding romances that was more than rumor.

In a recent national poll of high school students, the vast majority listed friendship as the single most important concern in their lives right now. Second place was a toss-up between doing well in school and getting along with parents. Money was important. Fourth or fifth came sex.

In a similar poll among married couples between age 30 and 50 there were similar results. Love and open communication between spouses came in first, virtually in a dead heat with love for and the

well-being of children. Career, personal growth, financial security, health were all high in the list. Once again, sex came rather far down the list of most important concerns.

In still another poll, this time among homosexuals and lesbians, meaningful relationships came in highest in a list of most important concerns or interests. Contrary to the popular myths about homosexuals, sex once again came rather far down the list.

All these scientifically gathered and rather reliable statistics contradict the impression common in our society that sex—meaning in all the above instances genital sexual activity—is our number one interest and most popular form of recreation.

All the statistics point instead to the fact that sex is indeed a nine-letter word. How we relate to others, the friendships we form, the love we give and receive, the responsibility we feel toward others, our own identity, sense of worth and value—all of these high priority concerns are to a large degree influenced by our **sexuality** and not our genital sexual activity.

Sexuality is who we are. Genital sex is just one of the things we may do because of who we are. That is why even a course like this can

give the wrong impression if we are not careful. Of necessity there has been a lot of discussion of genital sex. We must confront this powerful, natural drive within us and learn how to direct it responsibly if we are to integrate it into our total person. But it is just one aspect of our total person and just one aspect of our sexuality.

The major concern and the true meaning of our sexuality is **relationships.** That is what life ultimately is all about—forming relationships, being in relationship, relating to others as persons deserving our respect, concern, and help.

One special expression of relationship, within that very special relationship called marriage, is genital sexual relating. Even then the bottom line for that kind of relating looks beyond itself to others. The majority of adults polled indicated that having childen was one of their most important reasons for getting married. So much so, in fact, that this same majority said that if they had to choose between having no children and having six children they would choose to have six. This does not mean couples today want large families. Studies and the facts indicate that one to three children is what most couples aim for. But the vast majority do want children when they marry. The urge for marriage (and sexual intercourse within marriage) remains nature's way of continuing the race, even in our very sophisticated age.

Within marriage sexual intercourse clearly plays another very important role. It both expresses and strengthens the love of the couple. It is important, even necessary, whether the couple is fertile or not. It remains an important expression of love—and the physical drive remains—even into advanced years.

So people do not grow out of the drive for or interest in genital sexual activity. It is hoped people integrate this drive into the larger task of living and relating. It is—and should become for us—one of the many values, interests, and concerns that flow from our nature as either male or female.

Confronting this drive and learning to direct it responsibly is definitely one of your major tasks right now. It is relatively new, just as so much else about you is relatively new—your more adult self-awareness, your need to begin to make important decisions about your future, your need to become independent of your parents. Like anything new, learning how to control your sex drives can be bothersome, confusing, discouraging. It can seem like the most important thing in your life. Do you remember when you first started learning to ride a two-wheel bicycle? At that time that probably seemed the most important thing in your life—and it was often discouraging, confusing, even bothersome. Now riding a bike is simply part of you, who you are, one of the abilities you have.

Believe it or not, your sex drive will be, in a sense, like bike riding for you some day. It will become a part of your overall lifestyle—one capability among a wide range of capabilities, one priority among many others. It will be a part of you, but it will not be the most important part.

Chances are you have made some big steps in that direction already. The rough time tends to be the junior high years. Today that is when kids tend to mess up. If you got through that period with few wounds, you should be well on your way. Even if you were one of those who messed up during that period, you are now in a much better position to choose a mature, responsible direction.

As the poll indicated, the majority of young people your age have begun to see sex as a relatively low priority. Sex for most people really is a nine-letter word.

Who Needs It? (An Unfair Question)

We have seen how Jesus was a sexual revolutionary. He saw our sexuality as good and he saw sex as one important means for developing our full potential as human beings. So much so, in fact, that he saw both marriage and sexual intercourse within marriage as a way for us to experience the Father's love for us all.

But Jesus also looked beyond now to an endtime, a final perfection of creation and humanity. He envisioned a community, God's Kingdom, a family wherein everyone loved and received love from one another. No more enemies, no more second-class citizens, no more divisions between rich and poor, powerful and weak, black and white, no more using others in order to "get ours." He saw all creation as a gift to be shared by all, not as a prize to be won by the few.

That is why in that endtime Jesus said there would be no marrying or giving in marriage. Marriage as a means for learning how to love and for continuing the race will no longer be necessary.

We will, in this endtime, all have perfected our capacity to love one another. We will no longer need to procreate new human beings. All who are to be will be by that time.

So in this endtime there will no longer be a need for genital sex. But there will still be sexuality, males and females, men and women, love between men and women, special ties between husbands and wives, parents and children.

We will no longer need genital sex as a shadowy, sacramental expression of the Father's love. We will be experiencing that love head on, or as the Scriptures say, "face-to-face." The momentary pleasures of intercourse and orgasm—one of the greatest pleasures we can now experience—simply will not compare with the love and joy we will experience then.

Given that perspective, there are those today and throughout the history of Christianity who choose to skip the middle step of marriage in their journey to perfecting their humanness. These are the celibates, men and women who decide not to marry so they can devote their full attention to building the Kingdom and to anticipating it.

Celibates, including the priests and religious who vow not to marry, have the same sexual drives as all of us. They have the same need for close, loving relationships, including those between members of the opposite sex. They do not hate marriage and they are not afraid of sex. They simply experience a call, an inner urge to bypass this more usual route of marriage and parenthood to arrive at the same place their married brothers and sisters are headed. It can be rough, it can be

lonely, and clearly it is not for everyone. It is a special call, and as Jesus himself said, "Let those who can take it take it."

But the celibate life, again as Jesus has said, has its own rewards right now: "I give you my word, there is no one who has given up home, brothers or sisters, mother or father, children or property for me and for the Gospel who will not receive in this present age a hundred times as many homes, brothers and sisters, mothers, children and property—and persecution besides—and in the age to come everlasting life."

Jesus was saying this for anyone who would follow him, but it does have a special application to those who vow celibacy as priests, religious, or laity in order to better serve the Gospel today.

Jesus was also up-front. He warned that there would be persecutions too. Society would often laugh at his celibate followers, call them queer or perverted, put all kinds of pressures on them to give up their celibate lifestyle. Being celibate is not easy. But it is possible and those who pursue that lifestyle for the Gospel are special people in God's eyes.

1984 or 2024—You're in Charge

Right now and into the future you will be hearing lots of other kinds of discussions related to sex and human reproduction. Science now has the ability, at least in a limited way, of bypassing much of "nature's way" in order to reproduce the human species. There is conception **in vitro** (literally, in glass), popularly called test-tube conception. There is much talk about cloning. There already exist sperm banks. There is opening on the horizon the possibility for all kinds of genetic engineering through which a couple might be able to predetermine the eye and hair color, and other much more significant qualities, in the children they choose to have. Determining the sex of a fetus is already a limited possibility. Abortion as a legal-moral issue will not go away either.

All of these new possibilities demand a great deal of continuing thought and serious study. We just do not know what the long-range results of these new capacities might be. How will they affect the husband-wife relationship, the relationship between parents and children? Do they promise us eventually a disease-free, highly intelligent race or will they result in a new race of subhuman monsters? Who should control such powers? the state? the medical and scientific society? individuals?

Science has, in fact, entered into the realm where only science fiction like the books **1984** and **Brave New World** once entered. If you have never read those books, by the way, make sure you do. They were written long before you were even born yet describe with uncanny accuracy much of what is now possible today and which your own generation is going to have to eventually decide how to control.

All the moral implications of these new scientific capacities are another whole issue. The moral debate will go on for some time to come, be assured of that. Right now we just do not know how much of this is ultimately good or ultimately bad.

Finally all of this is bound to have some influence on how we understand our sexuality, our maleness or femaleness, our very identity as human beings.

There is no sense for you to get too excited about all this for right now. But as you move further into adulthood and assume your various roles in society, you are going to have to confront all these issues. So keep them on the backburner of your mind. You can start gathering important information even now.

Meanwhile, here is a little formula that might help you to remember for a long time what this course has been all about:

SEX =
SEXUALITY =
SACRAMENTALITY =
SANCTITY =

**SUCCESS IN BECOMING THE FULLY HUMAN PERSON YOU ARE
CALLED TO BECOME.**

We wish you success!

FOR REVIEW

1) Describe briefly the idea of the Kingdom of God.
2) Explain what the call to celibacy involves.
3) In your own words, explain how the terms of the formula on page 111 are connected.
4) Define: *lesbian, endtime, conception* in vitro, *sperm banks, genetic engineering.*